DISCARDED
from
New Hanover County Public Library

THE FINE ART OF READING

And Other Literary Studies

Also by Lord David Cecil

THE YOUNG MELBOURNE

THE STRICKEN DEER
  or The Life of Cowper

EARLY VICTORIAN NOVELISTS

HARDY THE NOVELIST

TWO QUIET LIVES:
  Dorothy Osborne—Thomas Gray

MELBOURNE

THE FINE ART
OF READING

And Other Literary Studies

LORD DAVID CECIL

DISCARDED from New Hanover County Public Library

THE BOBBS-MERRILL COMPANY, INC.
Indianapolis • New York

Copyright © 1957 by
Richard Michael Ritchie
and
the Most Honourable Robert Arthur James Marquess
of Salisbury K.G., P.C.
(Trustees of Lord David Cecil Childrens Settlement)

Library of Congress Catalog Card Number: 57-9359

820.4
C

Printed in the United States of America

To Cynthia Asquith

"You common people of the skies
What are you when the moon shall rise!"

THE FOLLOWING PIECES were written at various times
and for various occasions. "The Fine Art of Reading" was
my inaugural lecture as Goldsmiths' Professor of English
Literature at Oxford in 1949; that on Walter Pater was
the Rede Lecture at Cambridge in 1956; that on Conrad
is a revised version of the Ballard Matthews lectures at
Bangor in 1949; the essay on *Sense and Sensibility* was an
introduction written for the World's Classics; "A Note
on Jane Austen's Scenery" is founded on an address I gave
to the Jane Austen Society at Chawton; the essay on de la
Mare is a lengthier version of an essay contributed to a
collection in honour of de la Mare published by Messrs.
Faber and Faber; "Some Women Letter Writers" was a
broadcast. The other pieces are founded on lectures in the
course of my duties at Oxford.

Yet it is my hope that these diverse pieces, in spite of
their diverse origins, do compose themselves into a unity:
for the first study, "The Fine Art of Reading," states the
principles that in my view should govern literary appreciation; and the subsequent pieces exhibit these principles
operating in particular instances. I am more doubtful
whether the book is marked by that harmony of style

which should distinguish an essay in the art of letters. For lectures and broadcasts, designed to be listened to, are composed in a different mode from essays designed to be read; looser in structure and more declamatory in tone. Set side by side the two modes tend to produce a discordant impression. I have tried to soften this discord. But the task is a difficult one, and I may easily have failed. If so, I here acknowledge my fault and ask indulgence of my readers.

In conclusion, may I thank the Cambridge University Press for allowing me to reprint the lecture on Walter Pater, and the Oxford University Press for allowing me to reprint "The Fine Art of Reading" and "Sense and Sensibility."

DAVID CECIL

CONTENTS

THE FINE ART OF READING

"For the earthly beauty is a shadow and
image of the heavenly beauty."

—*Anon.*

After his death, said the poet Yeats, he would like to assume

> . . . such a form as Grecian goldsmiths make
> Of hammered gold and gold enamelling
> To keep a drowsy Emperor awake;
> Or set upon a golden bough to sing
> To lords and ladies of Byzantium
> Of what is past, or passing, or to come.

In fact, he applied the same process to his thoughts whenever he made them into a poem. So do all other creative writers. Are they not—like the goldsmiths— practitioners of a fine art?

Alas, this is too often forgotten when literature is made a subject of academic study. The academic approach and method was devised for other subjects: for philosophy, for mathematics, for history; intellectual, ascetic studies, concerned with facts and ideas, whose aim is the discovery of impersonal, objective truth. When they turn their attention to the fine arts, academic persons tend to treat them in the same way. With literature this is easy. For

literature is not a pure art like music. It also deals with
facts and ideas and can be studied with a view to discover-
ing objective truth. It is possible, for instance, to examine
Pope's works as an example of eighteenth-century use of
English; or *Paradise Lost* as a manual of theology; or to
read *Jane Eyre* in order to find out how governesses lived
in the reign of Queen Victoria. Possible, but mistaken!
For one thing, these books are not safe guides for the purpose. Pope—just because he was a genius—is a less typical
exponent of eighteenth-century English than are the
Dunces whom he satirized; Milton's theology, to judge
by the controversy that still rages about it, is somewhat
confused; and very few Victorian governesses, one is relieved to learn, led a life like Jane Eyre's. Moreover, to
read these books for information is not to read them with
the purpose that their authors intended. Art is not like
mathematics or philosophy. It is a subjective, sensual, and
highly personal activity in which facts and ideas are the
servants of fancy and feeling; and the artist's first aim is
not truth but delight. Even when, like Spenser, he wishes
to instruct, he seeks to do so by delighting. It follows that
the primary object of a student of literature is to be delighted. His duty is to enjoy himself: his efforts should be
directed to developing his faculty of appreciation. For
this reason, I thought it might be worth while considering
what exactly the development of such a faculty entails.

I hesitated for some time before deciding to do this,
because so much of what I had to say had already been
said by greater men than myself; and especially by Walter
Pater. Pater is a neglected author today. One can understand why. His mind is a little languid, his style a little
mannered, and he himself a little overserious. There is

something ludicrous in expounding the art of enjoyment in so hushed and solemn a tone. All the same, it is a great pity to neglect Pater. To a degree unparalleled among English writers, he combined the two qualities essential for critical appreciation: common sense and uncommon sensibility. So that not only could he respond intensely to the most diverse kinds of art, but he had the shrewdness to analyze his responses, and argue from them to arrive at a general view of the scope and nature of appreciation. As never before he made its first principles clear: he laid foundations on which anyone who works in the same field should build. I like to think that I have a spiritual predecessor at Oxford in Pater, unworthy to follow him though I may be; and to fancy that his shade, with its pensive glance and ghostly moustache, sometimes leaves its sequestered haunt in his panelled rooms at Brasenose to hover benignly near me.

I was further discouraged from discoursing on appreciation by the fact that what had not been said already about the matter by Pater and others seemed, most of it, too obvious to be worth saying at all. This, however, is not so, to judge by the number of so-called experts on the subject who appear to be ignorant of it. How many professional critics continue all their lives complacently content with a taste narrow, faddy, and inconsistent; while some academic teachers seem to take a perverse pride in possessing a taste so queasy as hardly to be able to stomach any books at all. Indeed, to enjoy literature as it should be enjoyed is a task of immense difficulty; requiring, in addition to common sense and uncommon sensibility, faith, hope, charity, humility, patience, and most of the other Christian virtues. It also involves a long and unhurried process of self-training. To begin with we must learn to start from the right place, to get the right line of approach. This means understanding what it is that we are approaching. We must have a right notion of the nature of a work of art; and, more particularly, must we realize that it is the result of two impulses. First of all, it is the record of a personal vision. Some aspect of the artist's experience strikes him with such freshness and intensity that he feels impelled to communicate it to other people. Gray wanted to write down what he felt and thought when he took a stroll in Stoke Poges churchyard one twilit evening in 1742. This, however, was not his only motive in writing his poem. People do not become painters simply because they want to paint some particular object. They do it because they like painting; because the creative instinct in them finds fulfillment in constructing a pleasing pattern in line and colour. It is the same with writers. If Gray had only wanted to put down the facts about his feelings in the churchyard, he could have done it with less trouble in prose. But he also liked writing verses. The creative writer is always partly inspired by his desire to construct a pleasing object in his chosen medium. Yeats, in the passage I have quoted, wants to sing of "what is past, or passing, or to come," but he also wishes to do it in a form made of "hammered gold and gold enamelling." This double impulse—to express the individual vision and to work in a particular medium—actuates every true artist. It is the union of the two that produces the phenomenon that we call a work of art.

A unique phenomenon: the result of an unprecedented and unrepeatable fusion of subject and personality and form. It is just this uniqueness which is the object of our appreciation. For in it resides its vital virtue, its aesthetic quality; only so far as it possesses it, does it exist as a work of art at all. And our task is to discern this quality and respond to it. If we feel so disposed, we can go on to try to analyze it into its component elements. Then we turn from readers into critics. But if we have not first perceived it accurately, we shall not be able to criticize it justly. Our first aim must be to see the work as it is.

This means accepting the limitations by which its individuality is defined. There is the limitation of the personal vision. I have said that the artist is inspired by his experience; but no artist, not even Shakespeare or Tolstoy, is so receptive as to be inspired by all his experience. Only certain things will strike deep enough into the fundamental stratum of his personality to fertilize his genius; only to a certain amount of what he sees and hears will he respond strongly enough for his record of it to be coloured and energized by his individual vitality. As a consequence, it is only in so far as his work deals with these aspects of his experience that it has aesthetic life. Every writer has, inevitably, a limited creative range. The reader should always be on the lookout to note the scope of this range. Nor should he blame the writer for remaining within it. On the contrary, he should realize that only in so far as he does so is he a successful artist. It was foolish of Charlotte Brontë to condemn Jane Austen for not depicting the full fury of the passions. It would have been equally foolish if Jane Austen had criticized Charlotte Brontë for a morbid preoccupation with personal emotion. Charlotte Brontë was not a cool and healthy-minded person; and the spectacle of the passions in violent action did not kindle Jane Austen's creative spark. It is no use blaming a writer for failing to do something he never intended to do; and, most likely, would not have made a success of if he had.

Equally must the reader accept the limitations imposed by form. There are critics who have condemned Ben Jonson's comedies because they lack the delicate sentiment and lyrical grace they find so agreeable in Shakespeare's; and who have argued from this that Ben Jonson was a coarse and prosaic person. In fact he was nothing of the kind, as anybody can discover by reading the *Sad Shepherd*. But the satirical type of comedy which Ben Jonson chose to write could not admit sentiment and lyrical grace without destroying that unity of hard glittering tone and slackening that unrelenting intellectual tension which are necessary conditions of its characteristic effect; and he therefore rightly left them out. Equally is it silly to blame Milton for describing the Garden of Eden in *Paradise Lost* without that vivid particularity of detail that is so delightful in "L'Allegro." The effect of sublime grandeur he aimed at and the classical, generalized style by which he sought to convey it, alike excluded such detail. Form conditions matter as much as the artist's personality does. The reader must learn not to quarrel with this conditioning.

All this should put us on our guard against starting to read any book with a preconceived idea of what it ought or ought not to be like. For this reason rigid systems of aesthetic law—rules of design and composition and vocabulary, and so on—are to be viewed with suspicion. No doubt all good works of art have certain common characteristics, like unity, pattern, style. But these can be achieved in many different ways. For, since each work is the record of a new vision, it must to a certain extent evolve its own new form and explore its own new subject matter. The so-called laws of art are only tentative generalizations drawn from the observation of particular works, and cannot completely apply to any original work. The eighteenth-century French critics who condemned Shakespeare for not observing the three unities are justly thought foolish; equally foolish is the modern reviewer who rebukes a poet for not employing what he hideously calls a "contemporary vocabulary." The only test of a book's merit is the impression it makes on the reader. If the reader is pleased, it does not matter how many so-called rules of art the author has broken.

The fact that any genuine work of art is unique should also discourage us from the seductive practice of ranking writers: drawing up a neat class list of the mighty dead, with firsts, seconds, and thirds judiciously awarded—Milton a safe first, Gray a safe second, Wordsworth just a first, in spite of some shockingly bad papers, etc. You can treat examination candidates in this way, for they are all engaged in doing the same papers and answering the same questions. But each creative writer is, as it were, doing a different paper which he has set himself. To treat them all as if they were the same and to mark them all accordingly is to misunderstand the nature of their activity. Our object should be rather, first to discover what questions the writer has asked himself, and then, in the light of that knowledge, to discover how far he is successful. No doubt, some writers are greater than others. Milton is a greater poet than Herrick because his creative imagination embraced a far wider and more important area of human experience in the field of its operation. But he is not a better poet in the sense that he succeeds more perfectly in his object. "Gather Ye Rosebuds While Ye May" would not have been improved if Herrick had tried to make it more like "Lycidas." It would have been totally different. When we come to considering writers of more comparable powers, ranking appears even more futile and irrelevant. Who shall say with any certainty whether Gray's "Elegy in a Country Churchyard" ranks above or below Shelley's "Ode to the West Wind"? Each is a sincere and profoundly felt comment on matter of equally serious moment to mankind; each is executed with a supreme accomplishment. Which one happens to prefer depends surely on the bias of personal temperament. Anyway, Milton and Herrick, Gray and Shelley are, as artists, all much more like each other than any of them is like a bad writer. Critics love dividing literature up into categories, distinguishing between major art and minor art, primitive art and decadent art, light art and serious art, healthy art and morbid art. There is no harm in their doing this—it can even be illuminating—as long as they remember that the only really important distinction is that between good and bad art. To a just taste there is more in common between Tennyson and T. S. Eliot than between either of them and Martin Tupper. For the same reason, it is a mistake to range schools or periods of literature in order of merit, though no doubt some have been more prolific of masterpieces than others. On the whole, however, the difference between them is between mode of expression rather than height of achievement. In itself,

Elizabethan tragedy is not a better or a worse form than French classical tragedy; it is another sort of form. As Pater said:

> The critic will always remember that beauty exists in many forms. To him all periods, types, schools of taste, are in themselves equal. In all ages there have been some excellent workmen and some excellent work done. The question he asks is always: "In whom did the stir, the genius, the sentiment of the period find itself? Where was the receptacle of its refinement, its elevation, its taste?" "The ages are all equal," said William Blake, "but genius is always above its age."

Genius—the distinguishing quality of the individual genius, that is what matters. There are as many different kinds of good books as there are different kinds of good writer. Each has something to give us. We should admire each in so far as he strikes us as good in his particular kind.

This further entails taking care to see that we are looking at a work from a point of view from which its aesthetic qualities occupy our center of vision. We do this naturally with a piece of music, for music is a pure art and makes no appeal other than an aesthetic one. But literature, as we have seen, is not a pure art. Books can be regarded as social documents, as moral lessons, or as pieces of biography, and grouped together accordingly; often with confusing results for the reader who is seeking to estimate them as works of art. Thomas Hardy, for instance, like the realistic novelists who were his contemporaries, was a rebel against the old-fashioned orthodox ideas of his age about sex and religion. In consequence, he has often been taken to be the same kind of author and, as such, has been rightly judged a failure. The man who opens *Jude the Obscure* expecting a sober, documented study of nineteenth-century working-class life, like *Esther Waters,* will naturally be disappointed. But, aesthetically, Hardy was a very old-fashioned writer. His conception of a good novel, formalized, romantic, and sensational, was much more like Sir Walter Scott's than it was like that of the young George Moore. It is only when we realize this and adjust our angle of vision accordingly—looking for similar qualities and making similar allowances, as we should when reading the Waverley novels—that Hardy's genius reveals itself in its full magnificence.

Again I have noticed that some admirers of Pope do not like Tennyson. And it is true that the moral and intellectual opinions of these two authors are very different. That characteristic Victorian blend of doubt and aspiration, high-mindedness and muddle-headedness, which Tennyson voiced so melodiously, is at the very opposite pole from Pope's elegant, Augustan rationality. This intellectual difference, however, does not alter the fact that, aesthetically, Pope and Tennyson are akin. Neither was an original thinker—that is why each reflects so exactly the mind of his period—and both were possessed of a delicate sensibility to the beautiful and an extraordinary natural talent for writing, which they deliberately cultivated to the highest pitch of exquisite virtuosity. They should appeal to the same taste in art. But to realize this the reader must be looking, first of all, for artistic satisfaction. A writer can easily belong to one school intellectually and morally, and to another aesthetically. It is toward his aesthetic character that our eyes should be directed.

So much for the right approach; but our apprentice-ship in literary appreciation is not over when we have achieved the right approach. We must also learn to un-derstand the language in which the work is presented. Not just language in the literal sense but language as a metaphor for the whole mode in which the artist expresses himself. This means, first of all, the language of form, the convention he uses. Failure to understand this has led critics otherwise distinguished and discriminating to say very silly things. Matthew Arnold, for example, calls Pope "a classic of prose," because he has never adjusted his mind to accept the rigid formality of the Augustan couplet as a vehicle for that serious passion and imagina-tive sensibility which he rightly thought essential qualities of great poetry. Again, the pundits of nineteenth-cen-tury conservative dramatic criticism refused to recognize Ibsen as a tragic dramatist because, unlike Shakespeare, he wrote about contemporary middle-class life and made his characters speak in modern colloquial language. At the very same time William Archer, who did know how to appreciate Ibsen, was denying any merit to Webster, be-cause his plots were, from the realist's point of view, fan-tastic and incoherent. Inability to grasp a convention different from that to which they were accustomed pre-vented both from recognizing that in their different modes Ibsen and Webster were great dramatists of essen-tially the same type, masters of high and somber tragedy.

Strenuous critics of the psychological and sociological schools often pour scorn on scholars for devoting their time to elucidating the conventions, formal and linguistic, of past ages, instead of occupying themselves in the glorious task of exploring the economic background of authors and analyzing their repressions. But without the work of the scholars, it is impossible to get near the authors at all. It is they who teach us the language through which their economic and psychological situations are expressed.

So also do historians. In addition to the language of the form, we must learn the language of the age. Past periods are like foreign countries: regions inhabited by men of like passions to our own, but with different customs and codes of behaviour. If we do not know these we shall misunderstand their actions and misapprehend their motives. It is the same with the natives of past ages. Poor Jane Austen is sometimes solemnly rebuked for snobbishness; and it is true that she has none of our curious modern prudery about mentioning social distinctions which everybody knows to exist, and which, in fact, most people set great store by. But this is because she lived in an age when social distinctions were taken for granted as a right and necessary feature of society. As a matter of fact, she is the opposite of snobbish in the true meaning of the word. She thinks it ridiculous of Lady Catherine de Bourgh to object to her nephew marrying the enchanting Elizabeth Bennet because she comes from a vulgar family. Unless we know something of the world she lived in, however, we may judge her as we might be tempted to judge a contemporary who referred to social distinctions with her blithe frankness. Some knowledge of history is, I am afraid, an essential preliminary to appreciation.

Finally, we have to learn to understand and accept the

language of the author's temperament—to school ourselves to look at the world from his point of view while
we are reading his books. This is much the hardest part
of our training, for our own personal feelings are so much
involved in it. Have we not temperaments of our own
which may well be different from his and possibly anti-
pathetic? Are we to treat these disrespectfully? Pride,
the sin of Lucifer and literary critics, rises in outraged
protest against so humiliating a proposal. Sometimes it
is our natural taste in manner or style which rebels. A
reader with a temperamental preference for the sober and
restrained will find it hard to persuade himself into a
mood to appreciate the grotesque extravagance of phrase
with which Browning so admirably expresses his natural
idiosyncrasy. Someone who instinctively responds to the
bold splendour of Hopkins' verbal invention may scarcely
notice, let alone enjoy, the subtle and unobtrusive felicity
with which Bridges uses the English language. Or our
antipathy may be moral. The puritan will recoil instinctively from Sterne, the pacifist from Kipling, the man of
faith from Gibbon, the infidel from Bunyan. Yet Hopkins and Bridges, Bunyan and Gibbon, Kipling and
Sterne, are all in their different manners and degrees
genuine artists.

He who aspires to be a man of taste should suffer from
a sense of failure if he does not enjoy them all. To do so,
however, may mean subjecting himself to a stern course
of self-discipline and self-effacement; he may have to
learn to subdue his tenderly cherished prejudices, silence
his garrulous self-important opinions, if he is to attain to
that receptive state of mind in which he can freely and
spontaneously surrender himself to the book which he has

chosen to study. Some people never even try to do these things, though they devote their lives to literary criticism. They take their first raw instinctive reactions as axiomatic; and instead of striving to widen their sympathies and correct their taste, they spend their energies in constructing a philosophy of aesthetics to justify these first reactions.

So stupendous a genius as Tolstoy lapsed in this way. He read *King Lear* and did not like it: his taste was for something more realistic and restrained. It did not, however, strike him that he was suffering from a defect of sensibility in failing to respond to what had pleased generations of cultivated and intelligent persons. On the contrary, he at once made up his mind, not only that *King Lear* was no good, but that its admirers enjoyed it in reality as little as he did; and he wasted much of his valuable time and intellect in evolving a theory as to how and why they deceived themselves so strangely. Such are the deplorable results of not learning the language of an author's temperament before sitting in judgment on him.

Of course, human beings are of their nature imperfect: and our temperamental inclination will, whatever we do, always impair in some degree our capacity for appreciation. Myself, I fear I shall never enjoy George Meredith's novels as much as they deserve. It is not just that Meredith's faults jar on me; twenty years' conscientious, if intermittent, effort have proved me unable to view his works in a focus in which the beauty and intellectual penetration, whose presence I do genuinely perceive, is not somehow fogged and distorted by my temperamental distaste for his particular brand of stylistic floridity. On the other hand, Jane Austen's art and views are both so peculiarly sympathetic to me that it is possible, though I think improbable, that I overrate her. But the fact that a man can never hope to be perfectly virtuous is no reason for him not to try to be as virtuous as he can. Nor should the consciousness that we shall never completely attain our ideal stop us from striving as far as possible to achieve a perfectly just and catholic taste.

In fact, we can broaden our aesthetic sympathies far more than we expect to, when we start to try. The taste grows supple and flexible by training. And though the pleasure we attain by effort is never quite so rich as that which comes to us immediately, it is a peculiarly pure and disinterested one—and touched with a special zest from the trouble which it has cost us. The spirit experiences an extraordinary sense of expansion and exaltation when, after a long and arduous process of self-adjustment, it suddenly finds itself responding for the first time spontaneously and delightedly to a hitherto unappreciated author.

Nor does our taste grow undiscriminating as it grows catholic. Greater breadth of sympathy makes us more detached, less partisan, readier to recognize that even our favourites are fallible. The more we are alive to remark the presence of the aesthetic quality the more certainly do we perceive its absence. How few authors, we note, perfectly fulfill either their personal or their formal impulses! Some stray outside their creative range, choose to write about experience which does not stimulate their imaginations; as Scott does when he leaves that Scottish life which he understood so intimately, in order to try recreating the world of the English Middle Ages which he did not know at all, and so can only embody in the figures of conventional puppets—elaborately described suits of armour with no flesh-and-blood human beings inside them. Or the vision itself may be confused by inconsistency. Thackeray urges us to admire Lady Castlewood for her noble character at the same moment that he is vividly representing her as selfish, petty, and jealous; Byron proclaims his indifference to public opinion with a loudness of tone that only betrays his secret anxiety that everybody should be impressed by him. In the works of both, the trained taste is quick to detect a false note.

It also becomes skilled to notice when an author's formal impulse does not find satisfactory fulfillment; to remark, for example, that many minor Elizabethan dramatists come to grief for want of some central principle of composition with which to integrate the varying elements of their play into a unity. The subplot has no organic relation to the main plot; the comic characters are drawn in a realistic convention, the serious in a wildly poetic one, so that it is impossible to believe in a world in which they are represented as existing side by side. Then there are the authors who do not recognize the nature of their inspiration; and, in consequence, try to express it in a radically unsuitable form. Hardy does this in *Two on a Tower,* where he takes a theme appropriate to a concentrated and lyrical verse tale, and then attempts, by filling it up with a clutter of conventional intrigue, to swell it out to the length required for a Victorian three-volume novel. Other authors again fail to perceive the limitations of their medium. This is the chief cause of Wordsworth's notorious inequality. He did not realize that to put a statement into verse form gives it emphasis, and that, therefore, it must be a statement that will bear emphasizing. As a result there is sometimes a comical incongruity between the prosaic flatness of what he says and the lilting song rhythm in which he says it:

> For still the more he works, the more
> Do his weak ankles swell.

Scott, Hardy, Wordsworth—these are all writers of the highest quality of genius. To be able to appreciate them is almost the test of a fine taste. But our capacity to do so will not make us notice their lapses less. On the contrary, the habit of disengaging the aesthetic element makes us the more acutely aware of the mass of lifeless and unaesthetic matter, in which it is all too often embedded.

However, the gain is immensely greater than the loss. To train our taste is to increase our capacity for pleasure; for it enables us to enter into such a variety of experience. This indeed is the special precious power of literature. In actual life our experience is inevitably restricted both by the limitations imposed by circumstances and by our own character. No one person can ever know in practice what it is like to be both a man and a woman, a mystic and a materialist, a criminal and a pillar of society, an ancient Roman and a modern Russian. But books can teach us to be all these things in imagination. Every reader is a Lady of Shalott, who, secluded in his secret chamber, forgets the hours, as he sits watching the endless procession of human thought and passion and action, as it passes, motley and tumultuous, across the gleaming mirror of literature.

And, like the Lady of Shalott's, it is a magic mirror. For all that it reflects is transmuted by the alchemy of art into matter for delight. This is very odd, considering how little delightful experience often is; how dull or trivial or painful, or unedifying! So also is the experience which forms the material of much great literature. In actual life it would be boring to live at Middlemarch, shocking to behave like the characters in *Love for Love*, depressing to look at mankind as Gulliver learnt to do, horrifying to find the story of *King Lear* occurring among one's acquaintance. Yet one enjoys them all in literature. Indeed, the worst is the most enjoyable. *King Lear* provides the most satisfying experience of the lot. How can this be?

It is no answer to say—as is sometimes said—that what we enjoy is not the subject, but the skill with which it is presented. Literary skill means ability to present a subject as accurately and vividly as possible. A distressing story, vividly and accurately presented, should therefore strike us as particularly distressing. Further, even were it true that a skillful presentation of a painful story did give pleasure by its skill, an agreeable story presented with equal skill should be even more delightful. But this is not so. *Twelfth Night* is not a more satisfying work than *King Lear*. We should not like *King Lear* itself better if Cordelia was saved and all ended happily. Rather should we feel such an alteration to be an anticlimax. The ruthless determination with which Shakespeare pursues his theme to its appalling close contributes essentially to the feeling of sublime exaltation with which the tragedy inspires us. In the same way, to descend to less elevated spheres of achievement, we do not feel that *Gulliver's Travels* would be improved if Swift liked human beings better, or *Love for Love* if the characters in it took their marriage vows more seriously, or *Middlemarch* if a group

of elegant and entertaining persons had chosen to set up
house there. A work of art is certainly not delightful in
proportion as it mirrors a delightful phase of experience.

This is a dark and paradoxical mystery, in whose shadow
lurks the whole question of the fundamental significance
of art. It is not for me to propose a final answer to a riddle
from which some of the wisest of mankind have recoiled
baffled. Apart from anything else, any such answer must
inevitably differ according as people differ in their interpretation of the significance of human life as a whole; and
so can never satisfy everyone. But since the ultimate purpose and value of that art of appreciation which is my
subject is involved in the issue, I feel impelled to offer you
a few tentative and incomplete thoughts on the matter.

Why then should we feel that the experience given us
by accomplished works of art, whatever their subject
matter, is agreeable; and not only agreeable, but also precious and illuminating? Surely the answer is to be found
in the fact that the soul is born instinctively desiring
order, harmony, beauty, but finds herself in a world disorderly, dissonant, and in great part ugly. In consequence, she is forever unsatisfied. The very best of our
experience is not so good as our dreams: our most exquisite moments are flawed and fragmentary. And they are
ephemeral. Even as we gaze the sunset fades, the apple
blossom sheds itself and scatters. It is the peculiar virtue
of art to present us with an image of perfection incarnate,
to show us some aspect of earthly experience, circum-
stantial, concrete, and recognizable, yet mysteriously
free from the imperfections which mar it in the real
world. The fleeting is apparently arrested in mid-flight.

"For ever wilt thou love, and she be fair!" cries Keats
ecstatically as he looks at the figures of the lovers graven
on the Grecian urn. And even the ugly elements in life
are made by the artist a means of beauty. Grief and horror, drabness and deformity—these are, as often as not,
necessary strands in the web of enchantment which he
weaves to take us captive. So that, when contemplating a
work of art, our desire for perfection and our sense of
reality are reconciled. We feel ourselves relieved, if only
for a moment, from the wearisome burden of our daily
dissatisfaction. For once we accept an experience unre-
servedly and with joy. Further, our joy is deeper in proportion as we are induced to accept what we normally
find unacceptable, in proportion as the vision, presented
to us by the artist, includes aspects of life which in our
everyday existence, distress us. For then his achievement
represents a more signal and extraordinary victory over
the ills of our mortal condition. There is a greater spiritual triumph in accepting Cordelia's sufferings than in
accepting Viola's happiness. Thus, tragedy brings glory
out of the very stuff of despair; in it we are made to face
life at its most baffling and dreadful, and yet to see it as
a thing of beauty and a joy forever.

Nor is this impression false, an opium vision conjured
up to dull and disguise the brutality of fact. If it were, it
would not be so deeply strengthening to the soul. No—
life is revealed to us more clearly when we see it reflected
in the Lady of Shalott's mirror; Shakespeare's view of
reality is truer than our own, as well as more beautiful.
For the perfection, of which he gives us a glimpse, is no
delusive daydream. Serene and changeless, it exists with
a far more intense reality than the transitory world that

we see around us, and which is, at its best, but its blurred and flickering shadow. Listen to Sir Thomas Browne:

> Whosoever is harmonically composed, delights in harmony; which makes me much distrust the symmetry of those heads which declaim against all Church-Musick. For myself, not only from my obedience, but my particular Genius, I do embrace it: for even that vulgar and Tavern-Musick, which makes one man merry and another mad, strikes in me a deep fit of devotion, and a profound contemplation of the first Composer. There is something in it of Divinity more than the ear discovers: it is an Hieroglyphical and shadowed lesson of the whole World, and creatures of God; such a melody to the ear, as the whole World well understood, would afford the understanding. In brief, it is a sensible fit of that harmony, which intellectually sounds in the ears of God.

For me, this is the most illuminating statement ever made about art. In it, as by a flash of unearthly divination, Browne reveals art's function in the scheme of creation, and also the mode in which it is performed. The artist, he suggests, converts the imperfect into an image of perfection, not by softening or omitting ugly facts—if he did, he would shake our confidence in his work as a true picture of the reality we know—but rather by presenting these ugly facts as the component parts of a perfect order and harmony. Further, the passage illustrates how any work of art does this, whatever its substance. Not some celestial strain of Byrd or Orlando Gibbons is it, but "vulgar and Tavern-Musick" that strikes in Browne his deep fit of devotion.

So also with literature. Any phase of human feeling,

however trifling, any point of view, however dismal or perverse, can be transmuted into an image of spiritual perfection—slighter no doubt than that evoked for us by Dante, yet an image of spiritual perfection all the same. The author may not have intended it to be, but he cannot help himself. By a sublime irony, not only pious Herbert and mystical Blake, but mocking Byron and irresponsible Sterne and worldly Congreve and despairing Hardy, are, in Sir Thomas Browne's sense of the word, devotional authors. For in so far as they have expressed their spirit in the harmony of a true work of art, they have opened the eyes of the soul to a sight of that divine and flawless essence whence she springs and for which, while her unquiet exile on earth endures, she is immedicably homesick.

SHAKESPEAREAN COMEDY

Are they shadows that we see?
And can shadows pleasure give?
Pleasures only shadows be,
Cast by bodies we conceive,
And are made the things we deem
In those figures which they seem.

But these pleasures vanish fast
Which by shadows are expressed,
Pleasures are not, if they last;
In their passing is their best:
Glory is most bright and gay
In a flash, and so away . . . .

                    —*Samuel Daniel*

I

"SHAKESPEAREAN COMEDY" is not the same thing as "Shakespeare's comedies." "Shakespeare's comedies" has come to mean all those of his plays that end happily. These are a very mixed lot, ranging from boisterous farces like *The Taming of the Shrew* to grave romances like *The Tempest* and powerful problem dramas like *Measure for Measure*. "Shakespearean comedy," on the other hand, means the great comedies of Shakespeare's early maturity—*A Midsummer-Night's Dream, The Merchant of Venice, Much Ado About Nothing, As You Like It, Twelfth Night*, with their precursors *Love's Labour's Lost* and *Two Gentlemen of Verona*; and these plays, though unlike each other in many ways, have certain basic characteristics in common which make them a definable, recognizable genre.

A genre, moreover, in which Shakespeare alone is a master. For the other great comedy of the world's literature, the comedy of Molière or Ben Jonson, is different in kind from his. It is satirical and intellectual, its aim is to mock some particular vice or folly; and it is rationally constructed so that every character and episode has its

necessary part to play in fulfilling this aim. Not so
Shakespeare's. The form of his comedies is loose, and the
different elements in it are not integrated by any intellectual principle at all. Here they are like other Elizabethan
plays. These were primarily entertainments; and any
element could be admitted to them which seemed likely
to make them entertaining. Even the line between comedy and tragedy was vague. All we can say is that in the
tragedies the dramatist seeks to entertain mainly by playing on our capacity to shudder and to shed tears; whereas
in the comedies the Elizabethan dramatist sets out to entertain by playing on our lighter, gayer feelings, whether
humorous or sentimental. Shakespeare's comedies are a
hotchpotch of all the different elements which con-
stituted "light" entertainment for an Elizabethan audience.

First of all, holding the fabric together, there is the
plot. It is never a probable, true-to-life plot, nor is it
meant to be. Shakespeare's aim is to take us out of real
life into a more agreeable imaginative region. The setting
may be called Venice or Athens. But there is no attempt
to make it a realistic picture of these places: each stands
for some exotic fairy-tale country, some Never Never
Land that appeals to the imagination just because it is
unlike the ordinary humdrum England in which his audience was living. The same is true of its inhabitants, at
least of those characters round which the plot revolves.
Hero and heroine alike are figures of romance, beautiful,
gallant, and witty, and with the charm of their personalities enhanced by the associations of high station. They
are kings and queens, princes and princesses, dukes and
duchesses. Doctor Johnson said, "A man would be as
happy in the arms of a chambermaid as of a duchess were

it not for imagination." Shakespeare clearly agreed with him: when creating a heroine whose charms are to appeal to our imagination, he makes her a duchess or something of the kind.

Again, the plots in which these characters take part are fanciful to the last degree. Since Shakespeare is catering for an audience who has come to the theater to be taken out of their own lives and not to see the sort of events that happen in their own lives, he chooses stories that turn on some fantastic hypothesis: a brother and sister so alike that, if dressed the same, they can be taken for each other; a man wagering a pound of his own flesh to oblige a friend; a girl deceiving her own father and lover in the disguise of a boy. And the emotion that actuates the chief characters is also romantic. It is love; again, not a realistic picture of the passion in all its troubled variety, but love in its lighter, more agreeable aspects, its prettiness and its absurdity—love as depicted by the court poet, and decorated with all manner of courtly graces. Blind Cupid shoots an arrow, his victim immediately forgets every other consideration: obsessed and exhilarated by his passion, like someone under a magic spell, he sets forth in pursuit of the beloved object. And if Cupid shoots at him afresh, he will change his object in the twinkling of an eye and without a moment's compunction.

This plot determines the general framework of the play, but into it are fitted any other elements which Shakespeare and his contemporaries thought likely to enrich and diversify their sense of pleasure. There is an Elizabethan phrase I read somewhere, "A Paradise of Dainty Delights." The phrase well describes the comedies, except that daintiness is not an essential. Any delight has a right to be admitted to the paradise. Broad

farce, for instance: this is confined to a group of characters generally of a lower social station. They are also
drawn in a more realistic convention than the hero and
heroine, caricatured pictures of English people of the
period. Their very names are often English: Dogberry,
Sir Toby Belch, Bottom the weaver, and Audrey the milk-
maid. Unlike the principals, they speak in prose and
make a number of topical allusions and jokes of a robust
coarseness. Such action as they are involved in is knock-
about and farcical. They provide an earthy contrast to
the ethereal lyrical atmosphere which trembles round the
principals.

Wit provides another strain in Shakespeare's comic
symphony: the quips and repartee and puns and word
play, popular among the clever and elegant of Shakespeare's age. Above all, there is the poetry. Poetry is of
the very texture of these plays. By its incantation is the
mood induced that may make us accept the extravagance
and fantasy of the plot. And it is poetry carefully designed for this purpose; light, sweet, lyrical, playful, it
never strikes the deeper notes in the poetic orchestra.
There is no brass in it: all is flute and violin.

Finally, and in addition to the music of the verse, there
is the actual music. The singers and instrumental players
were essential members of a Shakespearean company. In
these plays, Shakespeare gives them more opportunity
than anywhere else except his last romances. Moreover,
the music is made an integral part of the play. The songs,
as it were, crystallize the sentiment which is diffused over
the whole drama. In *As You Like It* they are wood notes
wild that tell of the pleasure of the countryside and proclaim its superiority to the disillusioning complications

of urban life. In *Twelfth Night* they sing of the fleetingness and tenderness and frail sweetness of love. So also
does the single song in *Much Ado About Nothing*. And
the fact that love is the motive force in these plays makes
their musical element particularly appropriate. For all
the characters, as much as for Orsino in *Twelfth Night*,
"music is the food of love." Indeed, it is easier to find an
analogy to Shakespeare's comedies in musical compositions than in classical comedy proper. Shakespeare the
comedian is closer to Mozart than to Molière. And his
descendants today are not the authors of drawing-room
comedy but of operetta: the sort of operetta that is set in
a Ruritanian court where the hero and heroine are a prince
and princess divided for two acts by some misunderstand-
ing but united happily in the third, and whose sentimental
raptures are voiced in strains of voluptuous waltz music
and relieved by scenes where red-nosed comedians entertain the audience by knock-about farce and broad jokes
and topical allusions. In type, if not in artistic quality,
Twelfth Night has more in common with *The Merry
Widow* than with *You Never Can Tell*.

Not that we can use the word "type" of Shakespeare's
comedies except in a loose sense. For though they all contain the same elements, these are mixed in very varying
proportions. At one end of the scale is *A Midsummer-
Night's Dream*. Here all the elements are present in their
most extreme form: the farce is more farcical, the fantasy
more fantastic, the relation to ordinary life even slighter
and more tenuous than in the others. At the furthest
remove from *A Midsummer-Night's Dream* stands *The
Merchant of Venice*. Here the plot is such as to make the
play only just scrape into the comedy category. The story

is romantic and improbable enough but, involving as it does the danger of a horrible death to one of the characters, it touches effectively on emotions out of harmony with the comedy atmosphere. *Much Ado About Nothing* runs a similar risk; the subplot is potentially a painful one. *Twelfth Night* and *As You Like It* represent the central norm of the type. All the elements appear in them, but not so etherealized as in *A Midsummer-Night's Dream* nor blended with melodrama as in *The Merchant of Venice* and *Much Ado About Nothing*.

It is to be wondered how so heterogeneous and incongruous a mixture of elements as is in these plays could ever combine into a satisfactory work of art. As a matter of fact, in the hands of most Elizabethan dramatists they did not. Their comedies, though sprinkled with humour and poetry, are too scrappy to be admired as wholes. But Shakespeare takes these flimsy bundles of scraps and, by the action of his genius, transfigures them into major works of art. Unity he achieves by suffusing his whole scene by a strong and individual quality of imagination whose distinctive characteristic it is to blend continuously humour and poetry. This makes the characters, though drawn in different conventions, inhabitants of the same world. Touchstone the clown is poetical, Rosalind the heroine humorous; absurd Sir Andrew Aguecheek touches us, pathetic Viola makes us smile. The texture of each scene is like shot silk, dark under one light, bright under another, as it shifts and shimmers in the movement of the drama. In Lodge's *Rosalynde* from which Shakespeare takes the plot of *As You Like It,* the heroine is always serious. By flooding her and the world in which

she lives with the quivering, gleaming, sparkling light of
his laughter and poetry, Shakespeare both harmonizes the
whole into one and makes us accept more easily the fantastic improbability of the story.

All the same—and this is the second aspect of his
achievement—he gives it substance and life: the substance
and life of the characters. We believe in a story because
we believe in the people in it. They are individuals whose
voices and manner we recognize: Shakespeare brings them
to life by a thousand little strokes of observation. But,
except in isolated cases such as Shylock, he takes care
never to do so in such a way as to be out of keeping with
his chosen comedy mood. The elements of real human
nature which he uses in order to vitalize them are all
elements that are not discordant with the general lyrical
key in which the whole is composed. They are made up
of the comic and pretty features of human character; the
graver and the more prosaic aspects are alike excluded.
"Rosalind," says Bernard Shaw, "is not a complete human
being. She is simply an extension in five acts of the most
affectionate, fortunate, beautiful five minutes in the life
of a charming woman." The same is true of Beatrice and
Portia and Viola and the rest.

As with the characters, so with their feelings. The
gaiety and folly and pensive sentiment of love are portrayed to the life; but not its pain, its mystery, its profounder influence on the character of the lover. If there
is a moment of anxiety or sorrow, it passes, and leaves no
mark when things go well again. Melancholy Antonio is
not very melancholy at the end of *The Merchant of
Venice* though he has been in danger of a dreadful death

twenty-four hours before. It is enough for Claudio to murmur a few words of apology to Hero for her instantly to forgive him for having publicly insulted her in the most brutal fashion. Nor do we feel either character unconvincing. For in neither case has emotion been so powerfully conveyed as to make its swift disappearance incredible. The characters are real but only as real as is consistent with the exigencies of the plot. The key is always light.

Within it, however, there is great variety of tone. Viola and Toby, Rosalind and Touchstone and Jaques, Titania, Helena, and Bottom—how many moods these represent! More moods, indeed, than can be found in satirical comedy. Shakespeare is in this sense truer to life than Molière or Ben Jonson. Wit and poetry, laughter and sentiment, farce and fantasy, even a touch of pensive pathos, chase one another across the surface of these plays as naturally as sunshine and shadow over a stream on a breezy day of spring.

And the stream is not a shallow stream. It is here that Shakespeare's genius shows itself most wonderfully. He gives his plays not only unity and vitality, he gives them depth. They make a profound comment on existence. Not a moral comment like the comedies of Ben Jonson! Shakespeare, indeed, has his morality. He disapproves of spite and hard-heartedness, he mocks at vanity. He approves faithfulness and generosity of heart. Good sense also: Orsino's sentimentality, Jaques' misanthropy, are shown up for the immoderate absurdities they are, in the light of the genial smile with which they are portrayed. Yet these moral judgments are, as it were, by-products of

Shakespeare's work, the involuntary and incidental utter-
ance of his natural preference, not the living center of his
inspiration. His comic vision reveals itself much less in
them than in his penetrating and cheerful perception of
the incorrigible weakness of the human condition. For
he uses the fantastic far-fetched turns of his stories as
parables to illustrate his conviction that all men, from the
highest to the lowest, are the creatures of chance and
circumstance. Wisely or foolishly, they plan their fu-
tures; always are these plans defeated by some casual,
unpredictable turn of events. Either something happens
they could not have expected, or they—generally because
Cupid has shot one of his arrows at them—upset their
plans themselves. "It is but fortune, all is fortune," says
Malvolio. It was true of him, it was equally true of everybody else in Shakespeare's comic world.

Shakespeare's distinctive vein of humour springs from
this realization. Man, he says, is comic because he is, of
his nature, a victim of illusions. This is obviously true of
his farcical figures. Pompous, conscientious Malvolio
imagines his fastidious mistress is in love with him; silly,
cowardly Sir Andrew sets up as a dashing young gallant;
fussy, illiterate Dogberry expects to be treated as a formidable officer of state; Bottom the weaver thinks he has
the ability to play all the parts in *Pyramus and Thisbe*
from the lion to the heroine. But the romantic characters
are equally the victims of illusion. Orsino thinks he is in
love with Olivia when he is merely in love with love:
Olivia loves Viola, thinking her to be a man: Beatrice,
who professes to scorn all men, is tricked by a few words
into giving her heart to Benedick. The more thoughtful

characters in the plays observe this propensity to illusion in their fellows and comment on it. But they, too, are victims of the very error they perceive in others. Benedick and Jaques do not realize that they are as absurd and inconsistent as those whom they mock so wittily. The wisest of the human race are those like Rosalind and Viola, who recognize their congenital weakness and accept it—who do not try to mold their fortunes but follow where fate leads them.

This strain of ironical wisdom in their creator gives substance and weight to the feather-light fabric of the poetry; and the humour that it engenders is that profoundest kind of humour that proceeds from a sense of a basic incongruity in the nature of the human condition. Shakespeare does not laugh at individual men because they are weak or vain or affected. No—he laughs at all mankind, himself included; because their very essence is a bundle of contradictions, born to desire something they will never get, or that will never satisfy them if they did get it; because they are a mixture of body and soul, each always at odds with the other.

"Taken as a whole, the universe is absurd," says Walter Bagehot in the most penetrating words ever written about Shakespeare's humour.

There seems an unalterable contradiction between the human mind and its employments. How can a *soul* be a merchant? What relation to an immortal being have the price of linseed, the fall of butter, the tare on tallow, or the brokerage on hemp? Can an undying creature debit "petty expenses," and charge for "carriage paid"? All

the world's a stage;—"the satchel, and the shining morning face"—the "strange oaths";—"the bubble reputation"—the

> "Eyes severe and beard of formal cut,
> Full of wise saws and modern instances."

Can these things be real? Surely they are acting. What
relation have they to the truth as we see it in theory?
What connection with our certain hopes, "In respect of
itself, it is a good life; but in respect it is a shepherd's life,
it is nought." The soul ties its shoe; the mind washes its
hands in a basin. All is incongruous.

But the depth that we perceive in these plays is not only
the depth of Shakespeare's humorous vein. It is also a
depth of sentiment springing paradoxically from the very
lightness of his intentions. These plays are the expression
of his sense of pleasure, ordinary straightforward normal
pleasure, not joy or enraptured exaltation. But pleasure
can stir profound reflections if a profound mind contem-
plates it. Shakespeare had such a mind. For the intensity
of his contemplation brings along with it an extraordinary sense of the transience and fragility of things human.
He draws a curtain and discloses to us a fairyland of
youthful carefree gaiety, all made up of jokes and song
and light love footing it with one another in tireless dance.
And then for a moment Jaques philosophizes, Rosaline
remembers her dead sister, Feste sings a song, and we are
aware that, with light unerring finger, Shakespeare has
struck a note that reveals he knows it all to be a shadow
play that will pass—alas, how quickly! As these bright

figures and airy music will vanish, so, we perceive, will the mood which they embodied. The pleasure of life is as ephemeral as a dream. All Shakespeare's comedies might be called "Midsummer-Night's Dreams"; and its last speech might be the last speech of all of them:

> If we shadows have offended,
> Think but this, and all is mended,
> That you have but slumber'd here
> While these visions did appear.

Such moments of realization are not harsh or discordant; the dance goes on, the pulsing, lilting rhythm does not flag. But the melody modulates into a minor key to be touched with a wistful sadness. The fair faces grow pensive, as for an instant there passes over them the shadow of their mortality.

II

Shakespeare did not achieve his full power as a comedy writer all at once. The mature masterpieces are preceded by two youthful unpracticed essays in the same mode, *Love's Labour's Lost* and *The Two Gentlemen of Verona*. Here, for the first time, all the elements are present: the romantic story, the wit, the farcical relief, the poetry, the songs. In it we find direct anticipations—first sketches as it were—of some feature or other in each of the great comedies. The disguised Julia, wooing another woman on behalf of the man she herself loves, is in Viola's very situation. Her conversation with her maid about her other lovers is a sketch for the more elaborate scene on the same lines between Portia and Nerissa; the clown, Launce, both in name and character, foreshadows Launcelot Gobbo. The last act of *The Two Gentlemen of Verona,* with its scenes in the forest inhabited by noble outlaws, suggests the *As You Like It* which is to come. The play is a creditable achievement for a young man. There are some pretty snatches of poetry and song. Julia is touching, Launce comic, and Speed rivals Jaques and Rosalind in his satirical observation of the lover.

But, like many first attempts, *The Two Gentlemen of Verona* fails as a whole. Much of the verse is insipid and undramatic; the characters do not come to life; and the plot of the story is too unlikely, even for a Shakespearean comedy. We do not believe in Proteus' treachery and still less in Valentine's forgiveness of it. As a matter of fact, treachery of this kind is inappropriate to the plot of lyrical comedy. The moral indignation it is bound to stir, if it is made convincing, is out of key with the general carefree mood of the work. Altogether, in spite of its occasional beauties, *The Two Gentlemen of Verona* illustrates the problems confronting the writer of this kind of comedy by showing us Shakespeare's failure to solve them.

Love's Labour's Lost, on the other hand, is a charming little success. In form it belongs to a different subdivision of Shakespeare's comedy from *The Two Gentlemen of Verona*: what may be called the *As You Like It* form as contrasted with the *Twelfth Night* form. In the *Twelfth Night* form, the action is very important; the characters express themselves in the turns of its development. In the

As You Like It form, the plot is a framework whose only
purpose is to hold the play together, to give it a beginning
and an end. The substance of the play lies in a series of
conversations which do not necessarily advance the action, but delight us in themselves by their humour, their
poetry, their observation of character and life. Shakespeare uses the plot to get the characters into some setting
in which they can walk about and talk to each other.

This is not to say that *Love's Labour's Lost* has not got
a unified subject or theme. On the contrary, it has two.
Such small shred of story as the plot involves shows us one.
The King of Navarre and his courtiers retire from the
world, more particularly from the world of love, in order
to cultivate their minds with higher things. The Princess
of France and some ladies arrive after a very short time.
The gentlemen, conquered by their charms, forswear
their first resolution. All this involves much comment,
sentimental and satirical, on the symptoms and arts of
courtly love.

There is also comment—and this is the second presiding
theme of the drama—on language and word play. The
whole texture of the dialogue is thickly embroidered with
flowers of speech: puns, conceits, elaborately worked-out
images. Sometimes these are set before us in good faith.
Shakespeare loved them and shows his love by using all his
art to make them as pretty and pleasing as possible. But
he also laughs at his own concern with language, and
satirizes the Elizabethan taste for it; delicately in the
characters of the King and his friends, more broadly in
Holofernes, the pedantic schoolmaster, and the affected
Spaniard Armado. This comic subplot, incidentally, an-
ticipates *A Midsummer-Night's Dream,* for it culminates

in an absurd rustic entertainment played before the mocking court of Navarre, as "the tedious, brief, history of Pyramus and Thisbe" is played before the mocking court of Athens.

In the main plot Shakespeare looks forward to *Much Ado About Nothing*. Berowne, like Benedick, is the philosophical gallant with a pose of cynicism. His relation to "the merry lady" Rosaline, is the same sort of elegant duel of the sexes as we see more fully exhibited in Benedick's relation to Beatrice.

As much as *The Two Gentlemen of Verona, Love's Labour's Lost* is clearly the work of a young writer. But here the young writer has found a form that suits him better. The plot is both more suitable to his talents and truer to the mood of romantic comedy; and the prevailing tone is so much lighter and more artificial that it does not matter so much if the characters are slightly drawn and the emotional intensity not very strong. On the other hand, the play gives him full opportunity to exhibit the distinguished charms of his youthful talent, his zest and frivolity, and exquisite foppishness of style. We may laugh at the frills and flourishes with which he decorates his every turn of phrase, but they please us all the same. And, after all, he is laughing at them too.

Furthermore, paradoxically, Shakespeare is enabled by the very formality of his design to sound, once or twice, a deeper note of sentiment than in the more obviously dramatic story of *The Two Gentlemen of Verona*. At the end of the play, when the lovers have confessed themselves to each other and all seems mirth and gaiety, a messenger arrives to announce to the Princess of France that her father has died. The news makes immediate marriage impossible. For a year the gentlemen are to be put on probation. All must improve themselves, and the mocking Berowne, in particular, is ordered by Rosaline to cultivate a softer heart; he must go to a hospital, she says, and see if his incessant jesting can amuse those in pain and suffering. Rosaline's curious command is expressed in too sparkling a tone to be taken with complete gravity. But the ground colouring of the scene is a little darkened; shadows mingle with sunshine, and by their presence show the figures as more substantial. As Berowne himself says, "Our wooing doth not end like an old play; Jack hath not Jill." There is no need for tears, Jack is going to have Jill in a very short time. But the fact that he does not have her at once makes the play more thoughtful, more unusual, closer to reality.

III

A Midsummer-Night's Dream is composed of the same elements as Shakespeare's other lyrical comedies: the fantastic plot with its exotic setting and romantic characters, the farcical underplot with its comic English characters, the wit, the light pretty poetry, the music and dancing, and all set in motion by the action of impish irresponsible Cupid. Yet *A Midsummer-Night's Dream* stands apart from the other plays in the same category; because, in it, these characteristic qualities are presented in a far more extreme form. We are shown the essential characteristics of Shakespeare's comedy stripped of any extraneous matter. It is the diagram and parable of its type. The plot is not merely like a fairy tale; it is literally an actual fairy tale with the King and the Queen of the Fairies appearing in it. The love that is the mainspring of the action is not just in the nature of a magic spell; it is in fact the result of such a spell. The farce is even more rollicking and pantomime-like than in the other comedies, the poetry more dreamy and gossamer. Moreover, the blend of incongruities, so typical of Shakespeare's comedy, here appears at its most startling. Cheek by jowl are found Hippolyta, Queen of the Amazons; Titania, Queen of the Fairies; and Bottom, the Elizabethan weaver. Classical Athens is surrounded by a Warwickshire wood, full of oxslips and luscious woodbine. Ghosts troop home to churchyards a few hours before a wedding takes place in a pagan temple. Theseus takes his Spartan hounds out hunting; Puck describes the rooks madly sweeping the sky at the sound of a gunshot.

Yet no work gives us more sense of being of a piece. None is in the deepest sense more integrated and harmonious. Shakespeare achieves this by two means. One is formal. His diverse material is fitted into a regular and symmetrical pattern. The characters are divided into three groups, arranged in three descending levels, of reality. At the top, there are the Fairies; in the middle, the mortal lovers; at the bottom, the rustic mechanicals. These groups are linked to each other by the fact that all are made to illustrate the operation of love; more specifically, they all form part of a story concerned with the lovers meeting in a wood at night. We see them separately in the beginning of the play: in the second act, they go into the midsummer wood where they are embroiled and set by the ears by the magic love spell. The climax of confusion is reached in the third act when Titania, the most ethereal member of the fairy group, falls in love with Bottom who, as his name implies, is the earthiest and most *terre-à-terre* character in the mechanicals' group.

After this the machinery of the plot goes into reverse. Gradually the confusion sorts itself out. At the end, all the separate groups are divided from each other; and their members at harmony among themselves. The main theme finds a comical echo in the play acted by the mechanicals which tells of how two lovers meet in a wood at night. The symmetry of the structure is also underlined by the fact that the mortal lovers are headed by a happy pair of married rulers, Theseus and Hippolyta, and the Fairies by a quarreling pair, Oberon and Titania. Lastly, the pattern has a center. The intrigue of the story is manipulated by one figure who, detached from the others, sports with their fortunes for his own amusement: Puck, Robin Goodfellow, the traditional English sprite full of rustic mischief.

> Those things do best please me
> That befall preposterously,

he says, and he acts in such a way as to gratify this preference. Yet even Puck cannot wholly control events. By mistake, he squeezes the magic flower on the wrong lover. And though he does not mind the resulting confusion, indeed he enjoys it, yet he recognizes the impotence of all effort, whether human or fairy, to control events. "Then fate o'errules," he says laughingly. Puck is the key figure of the play, the center around which its regular and intricate dance revolves. It is to be noted that he speaks the Epilogue. Shakespeare inclines to give the Epilogue to the character in whom the spirit of his play most concentrates itself. Rosalind and Puck each speak the Epilogue of the play whose spirit is most fully embodied in their respective personalities.

It is the pattern then, which imposes formal unity on the incongruities of *A Midsummer-Night's Dream*; but it also has an aesthetic unity; this Shakespeare effects by steeping the whole in one atmosphere, the atmosphere indicated by the title. The play is like a dream. Dreams are, of their nature, incongruous. In the waking world, it may be strange to find ancient Athens and Elizabethan England, Greek hounds and Warwickshire rooks, Hippolyta, Titania, and Bottom, all mixed up together. In a dream, it is the most natural thing in the world. So Shakespeare makes every effort to induce a dream atmosphere. Most of the scenes take place at night: all is shadowy, shimmering, and moonlit. A trance descends on us in which, without effort, we accept the incredible.

The execution of the play is as carefully worked out as its conception. Shakespeare starts by suggesting the atmosphere chosen, in the first few lines:

The. Now, fair Hippolyta, our nuptial hour
Draws on apace: four happy days bring in
Another moon; but; O! methinks, how slow
This old moon wanes; she lingers my desires,
Like to a step-dame, or a dowager
Long withering out a young man's revenue.
Hip. Four days will quickly steep themselves in night;
Four nights will quickly dream away the time;
And then the moon, like to a silver bow
New-bent in heaven, shall behold the night
Of our solemnities.

These regular harmonious lines are like a musical prelude, inducing the right mood in us. The word "moon" occurs three times. We are told that four nights—the period of the action—"will quickly *dream* away the time." After the mood has been established, Shakespeare proceeds to state his various themes, introducing us in turn to the mortals, to the mechanicals, and to the fairies. The change of atmosphere from one to the other is emphasized by a change of verbal movement. The mortal passage is composed in ten-syllable lines; that of mechanicals is in prose; the first appearance of the fairies is in a tripping lyrical measure. This variation of movement is sustained more or less throughout the play. The mortal lovers speak mainly in blank verse and couplet, the mechanicals always in prose, the fairies modulate from ten-syllable lines to rhymed eight syllables and lyric. At the climax of confusion, Act IV, Scene I, Titania speaks to Bottom in lyrical stanzas and he replies in pedestrian, conversational prose.

These metrical modulations are most important in the fairy scenes. Obviously the fairies are going to be the hardest elements in the play to make convincing. Their speech must be differentiated from that of the mortals if we are to feel them to be beings of a different species. Shakespeare does it mainly by the different mode in which they speak; light, ethereal, songful. When they appear, it is as if we heard a new instrument playing in the orchestra. But even the lovers speak in a more formal verse than in most of Shakespeare's later comedies, in stanza and rhymed couplet, or they converse in single lines that echo one another like the singers in a duet.

Lys.　The course of true love never did run smooth;
　　　But, either it was different in blood,—
Her.　O cross! too high to be enthrall'd to low.

Lys.   Or else misgraffed in respect of years,—
Her.   O spite! too old to be engag'd to young.
Lys.   Or else it stood upon the choice of friends,—
Her.   O hell! to choose love by another's eye.
Lys.   Or, if there were a sympathy in choice, . . .

This formality which would seem unreal for most stories, here has precisely the opposite effect. It intensifies and concentrates the evocative force of the poetry till it is able to lift us into magical regions in which we can accept spells and fantasy without difficulty. The whole play is, as it were, set to a music which lulls the prosaic spirit of disbelief to sleep.

The risk of this device is that it might at the same time easily lull the play's capacity to awake a human interest. This happens often in drama dealing with fairy-tale themes. *Comus* and *The Faithful Shepherdess* are exhibitions of exquisite poetry that steep the spirit in a dreamlike mood; but dramatically they are a little dull. The characters are no more than decorative mouthpieces through which the poet's muse utters herself in ravishing song. Not so in *A Midsummer-Night's Dream!* There Shakespeare wonderfully contrives at once to evoke the fairy mood and to maintain human interest. He does this partly by his humour. The spirit of laughter has a lively mind: always, she is noticing, criticizing, in order to find food for her mockery. While she is present, the senses cannot become lulled and dull. She is there all through *A Midsummer-Night's Dream* and at every one of its levels. Puck is a humorist—"Lord, what fools these mortals be!" he exclaims with chuckling delight. The quarrels of the mortal lovers are sharp with delicate comedy;

the comedy of Hermia's vanity and Helena's timidity and the gruff male embarrassment of their suitors; while, in the mechanicals, Shakespeare lets his humour have full play, ranging from the wild nonsense of the piece they perform to the humorous observation of character revealed in the scenes of its rehearsal. In these the essential comedy of all amateur theatricals is concentrated. All who have taken part in them will recognize Bottom, the man who wants to take every part, Snug, the man who is frightened of any part, Quince, the fussy ineffective producer.

This eye for character is the second means by which Shakespeare keeps his play alive. Even the Fairy King and Queen have their individualities; even stately Duke Theseus speaks with a personal accent—now gravely philosophizing, now condescending to his inferiors with the easy confidence of the great noble. Yet the characters are never made so human as to seem incongruous with the magical and dreamlike atmosphere. Though the characters are individualized, it is more lightly than in the other comedies. Hermia and Helena are drawn in delicate silverpoint: they have not the three-dimensional, richly-coloured life of Beatrice or Rosalind.

Oberon and Titania are individuals, but fairy individuals; their ill temper and jealousy are, as it were, human qualities reduced to a miniature scale. But, indeed, no one feels seriously; and the poetry, for all its beauty, is without the pathos which trembles through the graver passages of *Twelfth Night*. Is *A Midsummer-Night's Dream* a trivial work then? Not more than any other of Shakespeare's comedies. For it shows a profound apprehension of one aspect of human experience. Once again it is an

aspect associated with its title. Shakespeare, contemplating the motley spectacle of human life, seems again and
again to have been seized with the sense that it was like a
dream. "We are such stuff as dreams are made on"—thus
begins the brief mysterious comment in which, in his last
play, he seems to sum up his final conclusion about the
riddle of human destiny; and, more light-heartedly
stated, it is the theme of this, his earlier excursion into
Fairyland. He feels life to be like a dream, first because
it is so fleeting; second because it is incongruous and unpredictable. Everyone seems to move in a different dream
of their own invention. Nothing is quite what mortals
think it. Theseus expatiates on this in the last act of the
play:

> I never may believe
> These antique fables, nor these fairy toys.
> Lovers and madmen have such seething brains,
> Such shaping fantasies, that apprehend
> More than cool reason ever comprehends.
> The lunatic, the lover, and the poet,
> Are of imagination all compact:
> One sees more devils than vast hell can hold,
> That is, the madman; the lover, all as frantic,
> Sees Helen's beauty in a brow of Egypt:
> The poet's eye, in a fine frenzy rolling,
> Doth glance from heaven to earth, from earth
>   to heaven;
> And, as imagination bodies forth
> The forms of things unknown, the poet's pen
> Turns them to shapes, and gives to airy nothing
> A local habitation and a name.
> Such tricks hath strong imagination,

> That, if it would but apprehend some joy,
> It comprehends some bringer of that joy;
> Or in the night, imagining some fear,
> How easy is a bush suppos'd a bear!

These are sensible words. The only trouble is that, in their
context at least, they are false. Theseus is wrong to dis-
believe the lovers' tale. Things stranger than his common
sense could conceive of had happened in the wood outside
his city. Shakespeare, we infer, thinks that life is much
more surprising and mysterious than cool reason appre-
hends.

Indeed, though Theseus will not know it, beings in
whose very existence reason refuses to believe are coming,
within an hour or two, to haunt his palace and rain invisible influence on his future fortunes. Tired with
revelry and happiness, the lovers go to bed, the mechanicals pack off home, the great hall is left empty. The
moonlight streams in through the open casement; broom
in hand appears the elfin figure of Puck:

> Now the hungry lion roars, [he sings]
>   And the wolf behowls the moon;
> Whilst the heavy ploughman snores,
>   All with weary task fordone.
> Now the wasted brands do glow,
>   Whilst the screech-owl, screeching loud,
> Puts the wretch that lies in woe
>   In remembrance of a shroud.
> Now it is the time of night
>   That the graves, all gaping wide,
> Every one lets forth his sprite,
>   In the church-way paths to glide:

And we fairies, that do run
   By the triple Hecate's team,
From the presence of the sun,
   Following darkness like a dream,*
Now are frolic: not a mouse
   Shall disturb this hallow'd house:
I am sent with broom before,
   To sweep the dust behind the door.

He is followed by his royal master and mistress and their
gleaming train; flickering through the sleeping house,
dancing, singing, giving blessing, they depart. Puck remains to utter a final apostrophe to the audience on behalf
of the play of which he, not rational Theseus, is the significant and presiding genius.

IV

Technically *The Merchant of Venice* is a triumph. As
usual, Shakespeare takes the story ready-made and then
modifies it to suit his purpose. The story, *Il Pecorone* of
Bandello, was more fully prepared for him than most of
his comedy stories. It already has two plots—that of the
pound of flesh and that of the Lady of Belmont—so that
Shakespeare does not have to join two other stories together to make his play long enough. However, the

---

* This magical line is surely the first example in our literature of
the distinctive style of Walter de la Mare; as Iago's rhymes in *Othello*,
Act II, Sc.I, 11.148-160, are the first example of the distinctive style
of Pope; and the dirge over Fidele in *Cymbeline* is the first example
of the distinctive style of A. E. Housman. Shakespeare was so universal and seminal a genius that it seems as if he contained within him
all subsequent modes of poetry.

Pecorone story was not suitable for dramatizing without considerable shortening and tightening. In the original tale, the lover makes three attempts on the Lady of Belmont before winning her: obviously this was unnecessary and too long in a play. Second, the existing Belmont story was not right for his purpose. In it the Lady is a calculating siren who enters into a sort of wager with each lover that if he does not keep awake all through a long night of love in her company, she can have his fortune. A heroine of this kind is not in the vein of Shakespeare's comedy. He, as we know, substitutes the trial of the three caskets, a well-known traditional tale that he may have picked up from many sources. He also takes pains to alter the pound of flesh story to make it a little less unlikely than it might appear to be. The bond which, in the original, is entered into in a perfectly serious spirit is, in Shakespeare's play, made a sort of joke. We are not, therefore, so surprised that Antonio should have entered upon it. Shylock, too, whose crime in the original is motiveless, is by Shakespeare represented as having been often insulted by Antonio so that he thirsts for revenge and seizes the opportunity to take it. Antonio himself is portrayed as a victim of the melancholy humour so much spoken of in Elizabethan literature. This both gives him individuality and makes it more plausible that he should have risked his life in this curious fashion.

Having dealt with his story, Shakespeare proceeds to compose his play; and never have the peculiar problems involved in the double plot been more brilliantly solved. The difficulty about two plots always is to keep one from overbalancing the other. Here each is given its fair and equal amount of space; and never does Shakespeare stay so long with one as to make the audience forget about the other. All through the drama, we modulate continuously from the first to the second and back again. Rightly, they contrast in character; every advantage is taken of the opportunity for variety which the double plot affords. The Venetian plot is dramatic and semirealistic; and the Belmont plot is poetic and fantastic. The different manner which Shakespeare adopts·for each emphasizes and brings out this diversity. Yet he does not contrast his two strains so much as to make them discordant. The whole play has the unity and harmony necessary to any successful work of art. The Venetian scenes are not too prosaic. Antonio's words are touched with a dreamy sadness; Gratiano's sparkle with a witty fantasy. On the other hand, Portia, in addition to being romantic and beautiful, is also humorous and sensible. Though Venice has a different atmosphere from Belmont, it is in the same universe; people can move from one to the other without having radically changed their personalities.

Shakespeare, moreover, takes care to preserve the desired balance by a deliberate refusal to exploit the melodramatic possibilities of the Venetian story to such a degree as to risk its stealing the interest from the Belmont. We do not see Shylock's discovery of Jessica's flight, or Antonio's reception of the bad news that may lead to his death, before us on the stage: they are related afterward. Yet they gave obvious chances for dramatic scenes which most playwrights would have jumped at. But they would have stirred emotion of so violent an intensity as completely to obscure the soft poetic glow of the Belmont episodes. On the whole, the two stories are kept equal in scale, and the play relatively at the same tension till the trial scene where the two worlds meet and Portia, bright presiding spirit of the one, confronts Shylock, the dark presiding spirit of the other. In this scene, the dramatic climax of the play, Shakespeare displays his full dramatic force. But he does not end it here. It would not be in keeping with the lyrical comedy spirit to do so. The exquisite fifth act, all ashimmer with music and moonlight, slackens the dramatic tension so as to send the audience away in that mood of dreamy delight which it is the purpose of this type of comedy to induce.

The balance of elements so marked in the structure is equally apparent in the speech of the characters. There is no longer any question, as in *Love's Labour's Lost,* of formal artificial poetry that does not convincingly convey the effect of conversation and character. The style modulates from the realistic prose of Shylock, to the natural colloquial blank verse in which Antonio and Bassanio converse, to the delicate lyrical eloquence of the last act. But there is no feeling of jolt as we move from one plane to another. The verse is so flexible that it can drop to conversation and rise again to lyrical rapture without any break in its movement. Yet Shakespeare takes full advantage of its variety. It is by this means that he is able to suggest the change of atmosphere from dramtic Venice to romantic Belmont. Consider the end of Act I and the opening of Act II:

> *Shy.*   And I will go and purse the ducats straight,
> See to my house, left in the fearful guard
> Of an unthrifty knave, and presently
> I will be with you.

Ant.   Hie thee, gentle Jew. (*Exit* Shylock)
This Hebrew will turn Christian: he grow's kind.
Bass.   I like not fair terms and a villain's mind.
Ant.   Come on: in this there can be no dismay;
My ships come home a month before the day.

Act II

Mor.   Mislike me not for my complexion,
The shadow'd livery of the burnish'd sun,
To whom I am a neighbour and near bred, etc.

The rich imagery and musical movement of Morocco's speech following, as it does, the conversational end of Act I, carries us by its very sound and colour into the Belmont atmosphere. So, more wonderfully, does the opening of the fifth act. The tragic tension of the trial has ended in the humorous interchange between Bassanio and the disguised Portia. There is a pause. Then, like an orchestral prelude, we hear Lorenzo and Jessica's rhapsody on the summer night:

Lor.   The moon shines bright: in such a night as this,
When the sweet wind did gently kiss the trees
And they did make no noise, in such a night
Troilus methinks mounted the Troyan walls,
And sigh'd his soul toward the Grecian tents,
Where Cressid lay that night.
Jes.   In such a night
Did Thisbe fearfully o'ertrip the dew,
And saw the lion's shadow ere himself,
And ran dismay'd away.
Lor.   In such a night

Stood Dido with a willow in her hand
Upon the wild sea-banks, and waft her love
To come again to Carthage.

This mood is maintained by Portia when she enters. "How far that little candle throws his beams!" How wonderfully does this line indicate darkness and windless quiet! But it is more like ordinary conversation than Lorenzo's and Jessica's hymn to night has been. While preserving the mood, it coaxes us back into the world of real people and their actions.

The mention of the human beings brings us to the question of character. As we have seen, characters must not be very realistic in Shakespearean comedy or the fairy-tale plots will appear too incredible. On the other hand, they must be lifelike enough to make the story alive. Most of the figures in *The Merchant of Venice* perfectly achieve this modified reality. Examine the first scene and note how with a few lines Shakespeare has established Antonio, Gratiano, and Bassanio as personalities with their own individual idiosyncrasies of thought and feeling, yet not so powerfully and, as it were, solidly as to make them out of place in this fantastic story where one man pledges a pound of his flesh and his friend is willing to forswear marriage forever if he opens the wrong box.

Portia, as the heroine and the chief object of love, is more fully drawn, but in the same manner, with the same degree of reality. She belongs to the regular Shakespearean type of comic heroine, romantic and sensible and witty. But she has her own individuality. Rightly, as

heiress of Belmont, she is statelier than her sisters Rosalind
and Beatrice. Her conversation is a repository of that
smiling, reflective wisdom with which Shakespeare gives
weight to his comedies.

Por.   By my troth, Nerissa, my little body is aweary
of this great world.

Ner.   You would be, sweet madam, if your miseries
were in the same abundance as your good fortunes are:
and yet, for aught I see, they are as sick that surfeit with
too much as they that starve with nothing. It is no mean
happiness therefore, to be seated in the mean: superfluity
comes sooner by white hairs, but competency lives longer.

Por.   Good sentences and well pronounced.

Ner.   They would be better if well followed.

Por.   If to do were as easy as to know what were good
to do, chapels had been churches, and poor men's cottages
princes' palaces. It is a good divine that follows his own
instructions: . . .

Yet Portia is not too mature and intellectual to be the
heroine of a romantic comedy. Her first reference to
Bassanio, impulsively made and then half-withdrawn because she suddenly feels shy at having betrayed her interest in him, beautifully conveys the impulsive, romantic
girl beneath the demeanour of the grand Lady of Belmont.

Ner.   Do you not remember, lady, in your father's
time, a Venetian, a scholar and a soldier, that came

hither in the company of the Marquis of Montferrat?
  Por.   Yes, yes: it was Bassanio; as I think, he was so
called.

Nor is she ever too serious for the tone of the story. She
goes off to rescue Antonio from death not in a state of
anxiety, but bubbling over with mischievous amusement
at the thought of her disguise.

From the point of view of a piece of execution, therefore, *The Merchant of Venice* is one of Shakespeare's
masterpieces. In it one gets a sort of special satisfaction
in seeing technical problem after technical problem
solved with triumphant ease. All the same, the ultimate
impression it leaves is not so satisfying as that left by
A Midsummer-Night's Dream. For no amount of brilliant execution can hide the fact that there is something
ambiguous and conflicting in its root conception. The
story is not really a suitable vehicle for the effect that
Shakespeare is trying to achieve. For the Venice theme
involves the risk that one of the chief characters may
incur a horrible death. No doubt this did not bother the
Elizabethans as much as it bothers us. They were tougher
and simpler and, in a sense, more childlike. But for us,
for good or for ill, it is difficult to take such a story in the
light-hearted spirit appropriate to romantic comedy.
Either we do not believe in the pound of flesh at all; or,
if we do, it rouses ideas so painful as to destroy the play's
intended and characteristic mood. After all, the plot is
preposterous unless it is taken lightly. But, if we are
going to enter into it, how can we take such a plot lightly?
Certainly not if Shakespeare is going to exploit its dra-

matic possibilities. And careful though he was to keep
out some dramatic scenes, he undid his work by the way
he drew the character of his villain.

Shylock is the most fully living figure in *The Merchant
of Venice*. But this very fact makes him inappropriate
to the plot in which he takes part. He is the glory and
disaster of the drama. It is not that he is too likable. On
the contrary, Shylock is cruel and avaricious and revenge-
ful. Even his love for his daughter is mixed up with his
avarice. "My daughter and my ducats"—he does not
know which he minds losing the most: and it is only when
he discovers his loss of the diamond that he cries out that
he had never felt the curse of his nation till now. Moreover, bad as he may seem to us, he seemed much worse to
the Elizabethans. For he was a usurer and—in this play
at any rate—usury is looked on as being as obviously shady
as dealing on the black market is to us. It is emphasized
again and again that what Shylock dislikes about Antonio
is that he ruins the market for usurers by lending money
without asking for interest.

> I hate him for he is a Christian;
> But more for that in low simplicity
> He lends out money gratis, and brings down
> The rate of usance here with us in Venice.

Nor would the Elizabethans have been as shocked as we
are by the fact that Antonio had often insulted him.
They thought it right to be disagreeable to the wicked
and especially if they were acting out of their "degree."
As a heathen and a usurer, Shylock was an inferior being.

It was right that superior beings should keep him in his
place. To Shakespeare and his contemporaries, Antonio's
conduct to Shylock was as justifiable as Prospero's to
Caliban. Incidentally, we ought not to be prejudiced in
Shylock's favour by thinking of him as the victim of
anti-Semitism in the modern sense. The Jewish race is not
disliked as such. Jessica can marry a Christian perfectly
well if she becomes one too. It is the fact that Shylock
was a heathen and a wicked man that makes him abhor-
rent, and the Venetians, by forcing him at the end to
become a Christian, are repaying evil with good.

No, it is not because Shylock is too sympathetic that
he is a discord in the harmony of the play, but because he
is too real. He is a powerful picture of an embittered,
vindictive man in the actual world: the sort of character
who really would, out of hatred, concoct a horrible revenge and prepare to carry it out. Nor, though he is
odious, is he fiendish. Like other human beings, he has his
softer sides and weaknesses, his memories of his wife, his
momentary kindness to Gobbo: and though Shakespeare
may not realize how harshly Shylock is treated, he describes his reaction to this treatment so well that we enter
into his feelings all too vividly. His outburst is very hard
to answer.

He hath disgraced me, and
hindered me half a million, laughed at my losses, mocked
at my gains, scorned my nation, thwarted my bargains,
cooled my friends, heated mine enemies; and what's his
reason? I am a Jew. Hath not a Jew eyes? hath not a Jew
hands, organs, dimensions, senses, affections, passions? fed
with the same food, hurt with the same weapons, subject
to the same diseases, healed by the same means, warmed

and cooled by the same winter and summer, as a Christian
is? If you prick us, do we not bleed? if you tickle us, do
we not laugh? if you poison us, do we not die? and if you
wrong us, shall we not revenge?

It is not the only time that a great writer has been run
away with by one of his characters. Satan ran away with
Milton, Shakespeare himself was run away with by Fal-
staff. In all these instances, the author becomes so absorbed in his character that he invests it with an emphasis
and vividness inappropriate to its place in the whole work.
Shylock, whether odious or not, is a solidly drawn, realistic
character, with the result that he, by his very power,
creates an impression discordant with the general inten-
tion of the play in which he appears. He, himself, and the
dreadful deed he wishes to perpetrate, achieve a reality
inconsistent with the fairy-tale plot and the fairy-tale
atmosphere of Shakespearean lyrical comedy. Such a
flesh-and-blood character makes the incident of the caskets incredible. Just because we believe in him, we find
it hard to suspend our disbelief in Belmont. This shows
up sharply when the play is performed. Either the producer allows Shylock to make his full effect, and so destroys the general harmonious impression that the play is
designed to make; or, realizing this, he plays Shylock
down. He may thus achieve harmony, but only by failing
to do full justice to Shakespeare's greatest effort of genius
in the play. It looks as if Shakespeare realized the difficulty himself. In the last act, he strains all his wonderful
poetic power to flood the audience's mind with a romantic
magic in which the harshness of Shylock's fall is forgotten. But in the memory, Shylock reappears unforgettable

and terrible, and striking a note of dissonance which all the sweetness discoursed by Portia's musicians cannot drown. *The Merchant of Venice* is a diamond, cut and polished to a glittering degree of finish and set with a golden richness. But there is a flaw in it.

V

In *Much Ado About Nothing* we find the usual elements of Shakespearean comedy but disposed in yet another perspective and proportion. The general colouring and atmosphere look back to *Love's Labour's Lost*. *Much Ado About Nothing* is also an elegant entertainment whose subject is the merry war of courtly lovers illustrated by witty interchange and diversified by song and dance; also as foreshadowed in *Love's Labour's Lost*, the plot turns on the theme of two unwilling persons being brought to love each other.

In *Much Ado About Nothing*, both hero and heroine resist the passion. For different reasons however: Benedick is a detached, half-cynical humorist who despises sentiment.

> I do much wonder that one man, seeing how much another man is a fool when he dedicates his behaviours to love, will, after he hath laughed at such shallow follies in others, become the argument of his own scorn by falling in love; . . .

Beatrice, true to the nature of her sex, is actuated by a more personal feeling. She is not against love but lovers.

Marriage might be all right, were it not for the man who had to take the role of husband.

> *Leon.* Well, niece, I hope to see you one day fitted with a husband.
> *Beat.* Not till God make men of some other metal than earth. Would it not grieve a woman to be over-mastered with a piece of valiant dust? to make an account of her life to a clod of wayward marl? No, uncle, I'll none: ...

Their respective points of view show themselves in a special apparent antagonism toward each other. There is a perpetual jibing duel of wits between them. But Shakespeare indicates very early that this is only the symptom of a secret inclination for each other which they fight against just because they feel it to be strong. The story tells how, by a practical joke, they are led to realize their love for each other. We are shown the humour of the change. We are particularly amused to see Benedick becoming as vain and nervous and anxious to please and easily gulled and sentimental as the lovers he used to laugh at. Finally the two confess their love to one another. This confession is precipitated by the events of the second plot. Indeed, this is one of the reasons why Shakespeare needed a second plot. The other reason was, as so often, because the main plot was not substantial enough to fill out five acts. Though melodramatic, rather than comic, this second plot is also concerned with love, its characters are also courtly lovers.

Clearly, we are far here from the world of *A Midsummer-Night's Dream*; and not very near that of *The Mer-*

chant of Venice. Shakespeare mixes his comedy elements with a new proportion for his new purpose. The lyrical, fanciful side is less noticeable, *Much Ado About Nothing* is still a romantic comedy, "A Paradise of Dainty Delights," not a satire; but the delights are more civilized and sophisticated and earthbound. And it is to be noted that the play is largely written in prose—rich, imaginative prose, but prose. There is more backchat and wit and repartee than in any of the other comedies, and fewer lyrical outbursts. The general effect is more urban and indoors. Two scenes, it is true, take place in the garden, but much less is made of their setting than in the garden scene at the end of *The Merchant of Venice.* Hero says a couple of pretty lines about a honeysuckle arbour, but that is all; there is nothing like Lorenzo and Jessica's hymn to the moon. The general atmosphere of the play is that of a great Elizabethan mansion rich with tapestry and panelling; and where the candlelight glitters on the gilded sword hilts of the cavaliers and the jewels and bright eyes of the ladies, as they bow and curtsy to one another in the formal figures of the pavane which is played by the musicians in the carved gallery. The Elizabethan flavour is very apparent. More than in any other of Shakespeare's comedies do we feel he is drawing from contemporary life; that the talk of Benedick and Beatrice is a glorified version of the fashionable banter of the period. Certainly, to dress the play in anything but that of Shakespeare's period always seems to me to strike a false note.

The design of the play is very like that of *The Merchant of Venice,* the two plots run parallel till the fourth act where they meet in the big central dramatic scene of the play. The last act is a little different; for the intrigue is not so fully disentangled as in *The Merchant of Venice*. There, there was only the trivial matter of the rings to be cleared up. In *Much Ado About Nothing*, Hero's reputation has to be restored and the conspiracy against her exposed. All the same, the general tone of the last act of the two plays is not unlike. The dramatic tension is deliberately lowered while music and spectacle are brought in to please the eyes and soothe the nerves of the tired audience: the chanted ceremony at Hero's tomb and the dance with which the play ends. Alas, with the accomplishment of *The Merchant of Venice, Much Ado About Nothing* is marred by the same defect. Once again— though this time in the subplot— Shakespeare has chosen a theme incompatible with the comedy spirit. It is not possible, for a modern reader at any rate, to accept the painful story of Hero in the carefree, light-hearted, romantic mood with which it is offered to us. The behaviour of Claudio, her lover, is too disagreeable. No doubt, one should not worry too much about his believing in her infidelity on so little evidence: slanders of this kind are always believed in Elizabethan plays from *Othello* downward. But Claudio goes on first to repudiate her publicly, in order the more to bring her to shame; and then, after her supposed death, greets her father in the vein of playful banter, surely in bad taste even for an Elizabethan gallant. The truth is, Shakespeare has sacrificed Claudio to the general effect of the play. He starts him off as a plausible figure enough, young, fiery, and temperamental. We see how easily, and with how little grounds, he becomes jealous of Don Pedro, who is courting Hero on his behalf:

Friendship is constant in all other things
Save in the office and affairs of love:

Therefore all hearts in love use their own tongues;
Let every eye negotiate for itself
And trust no agent; for beauty is a witch
Against whose charms faith melteth into blood.
This is an accident of hourly proof,
Which I mistrusted not. Farewell, therefore, Hero!

Claudio here seems to be a first sketch for Leontes; a study of congenital obsessive jealousy. But this conception is never developed: in the crucial dramatic scenes of the middle of the play, Claudio is a flat, conventional puppet. He only comes alive again in the odious, heartless playfulness of the last act. And this is introduced, not because it is characteristic of Claudio, but because Shakespeare is determined to make the general tone of the last act bright and gay, in harmony with the spirit of the main plot. Not again is he going to fall into the trap laid for him by Shylock: he is determined to avoid stirring emotions too tense for comedy. He succeeds in this aim—but at the cost of making the Claudio and Hero episode incredible.

His divided purpose appears again in the character of the villain Don John. In the original Bandello story, this character is made also in love with Hero, and thus jealousy provides him with a natural motive for his plot. Shakespeare deliberately alters this. Don John is represented as actuated only by a general gloomy ill will and sour envy of Claudio's happiness and success. This is not so obviously plausible a motive: it makes Don John potentially a more interesting character. Alas, the interest remains potential. As the play proceeds, Shakespeare, possibly because such a character imparts too somber a colouring to his picture, tells us no more of Don John, who is just made to fade away and disappear.

Incidentally, we may note that Shakespeare's use of his source is here curiously similar to his treatment of his source in *Othello* some years later. Iago, in Cynthio's original tale, conspires against Othello because he himself has been in love with Desdemona. Shakespeare just mentions this, but insists that his chief motive is resentment at being made subordinate to Cassio, and his chief characteristic, sour envy of the attractive and fortunate Cassio. "There is a daily beauty in his life that makes mine hideous," he says. That Shakespeare should change his original story in this way twice over does surely tell us something about his own view of life. Men for him were not equal; he believed profoundly in moral hierarchy. The splendid, the beautiful, the magnanimous were intrinsically superior to the mean, the ugly, the unattractive, who should accept and recognize their inferiority. It was a basic cause of trouble in the world that some of them, like Don John and Iago, refused to do this and out of pure spiteful envy sought to overthrow their natural superiors.

This is a digression: for in *Much Ado About Nothing* we are not meant to concern ourselves with these deeper problems. Indeed, we do not. Here *Much Ado About Nothing* makes a different impression from *The Merchant of Venice*. Just because Claudio is so much more weakly drawn than Shylock, he does not bother the reader in the same way. He can be forgotten. The general effect of the play is harmonious enough. The tone of brilliant light comedy does pervade it: and such diverse sorts of comedy! Dogberry is admirable. Perhaps he gets his

words wrong a little too often, but how felicitous some
of these mistakes are! "If I were tedious as a king, I could
find it in my heart to bestow it all upon your worship,"
or "If a merry meeting may be wished, God prohibit it."
When Conrade calls him an ass, Dogberry rises above
mere verbal fun to attain a richer, subtler humour. How
touching is the effort of the ridiculous old fool to re-
establish his dignity in his own and other people's eyes!

Dost thou not suspect my place? Dost thou not suspect
my years? O that he were here to write me down an ass!
But, masters, remember that I am an ass; though it be not
written down, yet forget not that I am an ass. No, thou
villain, thou art full of piety, as shall be proved upon thee
by good witness. I am a wise fellow; and, which is more,
an officer; and, which is more, a householder; and, which
is more, as pretty a piece of flesh as any is in Messina; and
one that knows the law, go to; and a rich fellow enough,
go to; and a fellow that hath had losses; and one that hath
two gowns, and everything handsome about him. Bring
him away. O that I had been writ down an ass!

It is a wonderful stroke to make him boast that he has
had losses. He wants others to know that he belongs to
the important class which has enough money to invest it
and so risk its loss.

But Dogberry is secondary to Beatrice and Benedick
whose encounters are the most sustained example of pure
high comedy in Shakespeare. It is high comedy of the
Elizabethan age; which means it has its limitations. We
note these if we compare Beatrice and Benedick's inter-
changes with those of Mirabell and Millamant in *The*

Way of the World. Elizabethan Beatrice has a cruder notion of repartee than Augustan Millamant. If she does not marry, Benedick tells her, some man will escape a scratched face. "Scratching could not make it worse an it were such a face as yours were," retorts Beatrice. This may have been graceful banter to Queen Elizabeth's court; now it recalls the preparatory school. Compare Millamant:

Mrs. Mil. Sententious Mirabell!—Prithee, don't look with that violent and inflexible wise face, like Solomon at the dividing of the child in an old tapestry hanging.
Mira. You are merry, madam, but I would persuade you for a moment to be serious.
Mrs. Mil. What, with that face? no, if you keep your countenance, 'tis impossible I should hold mine.

However, schoolboy repartee only occurs now and again in *Much Ado About Nothing*. For the rest, Beatrice and Benedick show the merits as well as the limitations of the great age they lived in. If their jokes are cruder than our jokes, their language is richer, their sentiment more poetical, their moral feelings more refined. With what certainty does Shakespeare, in the declaration scene in the church, make the two modulate from humour to tenderness, tenderness to anger, and then back to humour again. Here we may see how Shakespearean comedy, so unreal on the surface, is yet close to the heart of reality. Benedick is one of Shakespeare's speculative philosophers, the more humorous brother of Berowne, the more sensible cousin of Mercutio, the more genial companion of Jaques.

How delightfully his irony plays over the things he loves!
He would not marry a wife who was not an excellent
musician, says he; and then a few sentences later when the
violins begin to play, "Now divine air," he remarks whim-
sically, "is it not strange that sheep's guts should hail souls
out of men's bodies?"

Like her sister heroines, Beatrice is the more dominant
figure. She is the same type as them, brilliant, resourceful,
warm-hearted; but she differs from them also as *Much
Ado About Nothing* differs from the plays in which they
appear. She is more sparkling, sharper, more mischievous.
Deftly does Shakespeare suggest the lightning swiftness
with which she lives and moves:

> Disdain and scorn *ride* sparkling in her eyes, . . .

> For look where Beatrice, like a lapwing, *runs*
> Close by the ground, to hear our conference.

And Leonato says that she often woke herself at night
with laughing. As later with Cleopatra, he indicates her
appearance and manner by subtle touches of this kind.
A glittering whirlwind, she is hotter-tempered than either
Portia or Rosalind: "Kill Claudio," she cries in the gen-
erous heat of her outraged love for her cousin. We are
not to take her words very seriously. The scene is a
humorous one, there is nothing of Lady Macbeth about
Beatrice. But Portia and Rosalind show no signs of flaring
up in this way. Still, that may be because the plays in
which they appear give them no opportunity. One must
avoid the fault of talking of Shakespeare's characters as
if they were real people.

Beatrice is real enough to vitalize the play in which she appears, and it is wonderful how Shakespeare, while giving full scope to her wit and high-mettled spirit, prevents her seeming hard. The diamond sparkle of her talk is relieved by exquisite moments of softness. After a mischievous flight of words she is suddenly seized with a fear she has said too much and then, with a charming impulse of apology, she turns to Don Pedro, "But I beseech your grace, pardon me. I was born to speak all mirth and no matter." Don Pedro tells her that he enjoys her talk. She was born in a merry hour, he says. A ravishing movement of pensive poetry—smiles and tears mingled—flits across Beatrice's mercurial spirit: "No, sure, my Lord," she answers, "my mother cried; but then there was a star danced and under that was I born."

Very subtly Shakespeare indicates from the first the two lovers' latent interest in each other concealed under mockery. The messenger arrives to tell Leonato that Don Pedro and his gentleman are arrived. After a few remarks Beatrice bursts out irrepressibly:

Beat.   I pray you, is Signior Mountanto returned from the wars or no?
Mess.   I know none of that name, lady: there was none such in the army of any sort.
Leon.   What is he that you ask for, niece?
Hero.   My cousin means Signior Benedick of Padua.

Though she is playful, she betrays her interest in Benedick. And he, when Claudio tells him that he loves Hero, says at once, "There's her cousin, an she were not possessed with a fury, exceeds her as much in beauty as the first of May doth the last of December."

VI

As You Like It and *Twelfth Night* are the two most characteristic Shakespearean comedies. In form they follow different patterns. *Twelfth Night* is the child of *The Two Gentlemen of Verona*: its action is dramatic and eventful and crucial to its effect. *As You Like It* follows Shakespeare's other comedy pattern, the *Love's Labour's Lost* pattern. Its plot is a light framework occupying as little space as possible, and is only an excuse to provide occasion for a series of scenes, comic and poetical, which do not, most of them, do much toward advancing the main action. Its source is Lodge's tale of *Rosalynde*, a charming decorative tale in the Elizabethan manner of decoration—all gold and silver, milk and roses, and green groves and Cupid's wings—as exquisitely florid as a piece of Dresden china. Shakespeare keeps to its main incidents; but modifies them, here and there, in keeping with the very different mood in which he conceives his own work. For Lodge's *Rosalynde* is a pensive, dreamy, Faery-Queen-like piece of Arcadian romance. Shakespeare's play is designed as an example of his particular kind of lyrical comedy, gay, shrewd, and sunshiny.

In harmony with such a mood, he omits or softens such elements in the original story as call for more serious dramatic treatment. In Lodge, the quarrel between Saladyn and Rossader, the counterparts of Oliver and Orlando, is an eventful, dramatic affair involving a proper fight. Shakespeare reduces it to a squabble. The end of the play, too, is different from the story in Lodge. There, the wicked usurping uncle is killed in a battle with the good Duke. In *As You Like It*, a messenger merely arrives to say that he has repented of his sin under the influence of a convenient hermit; so that there is nothing to stop the good Duke going home. Further, Shakespeare drenches his play in a quality unknown to Lodge, namely, humour. Some farcical and satirical figures are introduced, Jaques, Touchstone, Audrey; and the existing characters, above all the heroine, are made witty and humorous. They are also made human and realistic. Compare Phebe's description of the disguised Rosalind, with whom she falls in love, in the two works. Here is Lodge:

As she lay in her bed, she called to minde the severall beauties of yong Ganimed, first his locks, which being amber-hued, passeth the wreathe that Phoebus puts on to make his front glorious; his browe of yorie, was like the seate where Loue and Maiestie sits inthronde to enchayne Fancie; his eyes as bright as the burnishing of the heauen, darting foorth frownes with disdaine, and smiles with fauor, lightning such lookes as would enflame desire, were shee wrapt in the Circle of the fronzen Zoane; in his cheekes the vermilion teinture of the Rose flourished upon naturall Alabaster, the blush of the Morne and Lunaes siluer showe were so liuely portrayed, that the Troyan that fils out wine to Iupiter was not halfe so beautifull; his face was full of pleasance, and all reft of his liniaments proportioned with such excellence, as Phoebe was fettred in the sweetnes of his feature.

This pretty piece of formal decoration has not much relation to anybody's idea of a real youth. The corresponding speech in Shakespeare is vividy realistic:

It is a pretty youth: not very pretty:
But; sure, he's proud; and yet his pride becomes him:
He'll make a proper man: the best thing in him
Is his complexion; and faster than his tongue
Did make offence his eye did heal it up.
He is not very tall; yet for his years he's tall:
His leg is but so so; and yet 'tis well:
There was a pretty redness in his lip,
A little riper and more lusty red
Than that mix'd in his cheek; 'twas just the difference
Betwixt the constant red and mingled damask.

Shakespeare also takes pains to soften those features in his hero which might make him unsympathetic. Rossader, in Lodge, hesitates to save his brother because he wishes to inherit his fortune in order to be in a better position to marry Rosalynde. Shakespeare's Orlando, on the other hand, is only held back for a brief moment by an irrepressible feeling of resentment at the dreadful injuries he has received at Oliver's hands. Finally, Shakespeare's play is endued by a deeper, more spiritual unity than belongs to Lodge's story. For the whole play is made to illustrate two presiding themes.

The first is Shakespeare's usual comedy theme of light romantic love. Here he is not out to show its comic consequences in action as in *Much Ado About Nothing* and *A Midsummer-Night's Dream*. *As You Like It* is not concerned with action: love in it is primarily a subject for talk. In the scenes between Rosalind and Orlando or Silvius and Phebe, Shakespeare exhibits its poetry, its sweetness, its delicate fantasy. But he mocks it too, in various moods of mockery. Rosalind does it, lightly, delicately, subtly.

Ros. There is none of my uncle's marks upon you: he taught me how to know a man in love; in which cage of rushes I am sure you are not prisoner.

Orl. What were his marks?

Ros. A lean cheek, which you have not; a blue eye and sunken, which you have not; an unquestionable spirit, which you have not; a beard neglected, which you have not: but I pardon you for that, for, simply, your having in beard is a younger brother's revenue. Then, your hose should be ungartered, your bonnet unbanded, your sleeve unbuttoned, your shoe untied, and everything about you demonstrating a careless desolation. . . .

or

Ros. The poor world is almost six thousand years old, and in all this time there was not any man died in his own person, *videlicet,* in a love-cause. Troilus had his brains dashed out with a Grecian club; yet he did what he could to die before, and he is one of the patterns of love. Leander, he would have lived many a fair year, though Hero had turned nun, if it had not been for a hot midsummer night; for, good youth, he went but forth to wash him in the Hellespont, and being taken with the cramp was drowned; and the foolish coroners of that age found it was "Hero of Sestos". But these are all lies; men have died from time to time, and worms have eaten them, but not for love.

It is more farcically mocked by Touchstone in a sort of parody of the elegant and sentimental entanglements of the main characters.

I remember, when I was
in love I broke my sword upon a stone, and bid him take
that for coming a-night to Jane Smile; and I remember
the kissing of her batler and the cow's dugs that her pretty
chopped hands had milked; and I remember the wooing
of a peascod instead of her, from whom I took two cods,
and giving her them again, said with weeping tears,
"Wear these for my sake." We that are true lovers run
into strange capers; but as all is mortal in nature, so is all
nature in love mortal in folly.

The second and more specifically characteristic theme
of *As You Like It* is pastoral. Throughout the play,
Shakespeare contrasts the corrupt and sophisticated life
of town and court with the free, fresh, natural life of the
greenwood: and this, in its turn, is represented as a sur-
vival of the good life of the antique world in the Golden
Age, of which no trace is left in court and city.

> *Orl.*   O good old man! how well in thee appears
> The constant service of the antique world,
> When service sweat for duty, not for meed!
> Thou art not for the fashion of these times,
> Where none will sweat but for promotion,
> And having that, do choke their service up
> Even with the having: . . .

The contrast between forest and court is expanded more
fully in the Duke's speech:

> Hath not old custom made this life more sweet
> Than that of painted pomp? Are not these woods

More free from peril than the envious court?
Here feel we but the penalty of Adam,
The seasons' difference; as, the icy fang
And churlish chiding of the winter's wind,
Which, when it bites and blows upon my body,
Even till I shrink with cold, I smile and say
"This is no flattery: these are counsellors
That feelingly persuade me what I am."
Sweet are the uses of adversity,
Which like the toad, ugly and venomous,
Wears yet a precious jewel in his head;
And this our life exempt from public haunt,
Finds tongues in trees, books in the running brook,
Sermons in stones, and good in every thing.

It appears in its most concentrated form in the songs
which, as in all Shakespeare's mature works, distil into
their lyrical essence, the pervading sentiment of the play
in which they appear.

> Who doth ambition shun.
> And loves to live i' the sun,
> Seeking the food he eats,
> And pleas'd with what he gets,
> Come hither, come hither, come hither:
> Here shall he see
> No enemy
> But winter and rough weather.

Neither of these themes is very original. In fact, both
are commonplaces of the lyrics of the time, both are
found in Lodge's story. Nor does Shakespeare treat them

very seriously. To do so would go against the carefree
spirit of his comedies. How little serious he is appears in
the picture of the natural world he presents to us. The
Forest of Arden is not like any forest human eyes have
seen. No real forest has oaks and palms and olives growing in it, and doves and lions and serpents as natives of its
glades. Nor, except in the songs, is there any rough
weather in Arden: the sun seems to shine perpetually
there. And its inhabitants have nothing to do, apparently,
except to walk about and talk. The shepherds mention
their sheep but seem in no hurry to minister to them. In
fact, Shakespeare is not describing a region in the real
world at all. Yet once more he has conjured up for our
pleasure a Never Never Land, as unrelated to reality as
Titania's wood. Even the talk of the wicked world of
civilization is not to be taken very gravely. The characters are perfectly happy to go back to it, when the play
ends. But it is pleasant for them and for the audience to
indulge for a space in this idle smiling dream of an ideal
life of nature, the green and golden scene of some Giorgione pastoral painting.

A further charm is added to it by the delightfully
incongruous mixture of human beings we find there. The
exiled Duke, and his daughter disguised as a boy, and the
melancholy, philosophical Jaques forgather under the
greenwood tree, in company with a shepherd and shepherdess of classic pastoral, Silvius and Phebe, and the
Warwickshire rustics, Audrey and the clown. Now
shaded by an exotic palm tree, now by an English oak,
they stroll about and jest and sing and make love, "fleeting
the time carelessly as they did in the Golden Age." In-

deed, the whole play is a picture of the Golden Age, whither all these motley and delightful human beings have repaired to "lose and neglect the creeping hours of time." It is this conception which is the center of the play: this it is for which the plot provides its slight, perfunctory framework. Perhaps it is a thought too perfunctory! If one must criticize this exquisite entertainment, it is that here and there Shakespeare shows himself a little careless about making the action convincing. The hermit is too hastily brought in to bring about a happy end. The truth was that Shakespeare wanted to get his characters into the forest at the beginning and out of it at the end. He does both as quickly as possible and by any means at his disposal.

But these means do not destroy the harmony of the play, as do the improbabilities in the plot of *Much Ado About Nothing*. They occupy too little space for one thing and, for another, the general atmosphere is so fanciful and irresponsible that we swallow them as easily as we do the incidents in an opera of Mozart. For the rest, the play is a "Paradise of Dainty Delights" indeed, all endued with the same individual flavour. The flavour blends, in a manner peculiar to itself, those two elements of comedy and poetry which distinguish all Shakespeare's plays of this kind. It is a light poetry that is as far from the dreamy magic of *A Midsummer-Night's Dream* as it is from the wistful pathos of *Twelfth Night*. A great deal of the dialogue is in prose; and prose and verse alike have a crisp, elegant quality that excludes magic and pathos. For all its fantastic irresponsibility of character and setting, *As You Like It* is full of a golden common sense. All through, extravagance of feeling and action are gaily laughed at: the extravagance of lovers of course, their sentimentality and solemnity, and the neglect of the common demands of life which their passion involves them in.

And equally with the extravagance of love, *As You Like It* mocks at the extravagance of theoretical philosophers. This is most subtly and elaborately done in the figure of Jaques. The basis of his character is a typical figure of Elizabethan literature, the melancholy man. According to Elizabethan psychology, every man is made up of four humours. In the perfect character, they blend equally. In the imperfect, one predominates over the others. In the case of Jaques, the melancholy humour is predominating. He is the misanthrope, the pessimist, who thinks he has seen through all human activities to perceive their ultimate vanity. In Shakespeare's hands, however, he becomes not a type but a memorable individual. Jaques is a wise man in his way. His two big speeches on the hunted stag and on the seven ages of man are full of truth. Jaques is not to be easily answered when he remarks that the hunted stag is not enjoying the Golden Age as his hunters are; and in the Seven Ages speech, he points out with unforgettable force how man is conditioned all through his life by the particular circumstances of the age he has arrived at. All the same, Jaques, taken as a whole, is a subject for irony on Shakespeare's part; because he is unbalanced. He has been, we are told, a wild libertine. Now he has reacted equally violently against the pleasures of the world. He does not follow the golden mean. The golden mean is the right standard for life in a golden age. What is the good of his repining? "And your experience makes you sad!" says sensible Rosalind to him. "I had rather have a fool to make me merry than experience to make me sad." Shakespeare leaves us in no doubt that he is of Rosalind's mind.

Jaques is not the only philosopher in the play. There is Corin, the rustic philosopher:

Touch. Hast any philosophy in thee, shepherd?
Cor. No more but that I know the more one sickens the worse at ease he is; and that he that wants money, means, and content, is without three good friends; that the property of rain is to wet, and fire to burn; that good pasture makes fat sheep, and that a great cause of the night is lack of the sun; that he that hath learned no wit by nature nor art may complain of good breeding, or comes of a very dull kindred.

There is Touchstone the fool who caricatures all professional philosophers as he also caricatures the absurdities of serious mankind:

Truly, shepherd, in respect of itself, it is a good life; but in respect that it is a shepherd's life, it is naught. In respect that it is solitary, I like it very well; but in respect that it is private, it is a very vile life. Now, in respect it is in the fields, it pleaseth me well; but in respect it is not in the court, it is tedious. As it is a spare life, look you, it fits my humour well; but as there is no more plenty in it, it goes much against my stomach.

But even Touchstone cannot caricature Rosalind. More than any other of Shakespeare's heroines, she is the genius and presiding spirit of the play. In her person she expresses its paradox. Her situation—a princess in a wood disguised as a shepherd boy—is as fantastic as can be. Yet no character so breathes humour and good sense, for she realizes the lesson that lies at the center of all Shakepeare's comic vision. Mankind, he feels, cannot hope to dominate circumstances; at every turn, they are inevitably the creatures of chance, and Cupid. But the sensible person realizes this and makes allowances for it and will accept the human situation and is not dismayed by it.

Rosalind is of the same family as Shakespeare's other heroines. Like Beatrice and Portia and Viola, she is gay and sensible and adventurous and independent. But she is no more identical with her sisters than they are identical with each other. A princess of the greenwood, she partakes both of the qualities of her birth and her environment. Her wit is playful and whimsical, delighting in comical unexpected similes and flights of fancy. She dwells, she says, "on the edge of the forest like a fringe upon a petticoat." "Look here what I found on a palm-tree," she remarks on finding one of Orlando's verses to her. "I was never so berhymed since Pythagoras' time, that I was an Irish rat, which I can hardly remember." Or she confesses to Celia:

O coz, coz, coz, my pretty little coz, that thou didst know how many fathom deep I am in love! But it cannot be sounded: my affection hath an unknown bottom, like the bay of Portugal.

Shakespeare's heroines are objects of love and drawn in the light of this fact. Shakespeare's emphasis is on their charm; a charm which tells us much about the ideal of feminine attractiveness current in his period. Latter-day feminists talk as if women in the sixteenth and seventeenth centuries were oppressed slaves. Surely if this was so, male authors would give them the qualities appropriate to an oppressed slave. But certainly Shakespeare does not. His women dominate the action and are wiser than the men. Even while they love them, they laugh at them and save them. Nor would it seem were they so far from reality as we might expect. Listen to Dorothy Osborne, thirty-odd years later, describing the qualities she required in a husband:

He should not be so much a country gentleman as to understand nothing but hawks and dogs, and to be fonder of either than of his wife; nor of the next sort of them, whose aim reaches no further than to be Justice of Peace, and once in his life High Sheriff, who reads no book but Statutes and studies nothing but how to make a speech interlarded with Latin, that may amaze his disagreeing poor neighbours, and fright them rather than persuade them into quietness. He must not be a thing that began the world in a free school, was sent from thence to the University, and is at his farthest when he reaches the Inns of Court; has no acquaintance but those of his form in these places, speaks the French he has picked out of old laws, and admires nothing but the stories he has heard of the revels that were kept there before his time. He must not be a Town-gallant neither, that lives in a tavern and an ordinary, that cannot imagine how an hour should be spent without company, unless it be in sleeping, that makes court to all the women he sees, thinks they believe him, and is laughed at equally. Nor a travelled monsieur whose head is all feather inside and outside; that can talk of nothing but dances and duels, and has courage enough to wear slashes when everybody else dies with cold to see him. He must not be a fool of no sort, nor peevish ill-natured, nor proud nor covetous, and to all this must be added he must love me.

Is not this the very accent of Rosalind or Portia? The great lady of that age was no slave. It would have been odd if she were, living as she did, in the days of Queen Elizabeth I and Mary Queen of Scots.

Anyway—whether they are true to Elizabethan nature or not—these heroines are true to Shakespeare's comic vision. They concentrate in themselves the two strains which distinguish it, romance and good sense. They are at once the wisest and shrewdest characters in the plays, and also the radiant object of that romantic love in whose light they are bathed. Shakespeare's comedy heroines are the finest compliment ever paid to the female sex by an English writer.

VII

It is quite right that *Twelfth Night* should be the last of Shakespeare's lyrical comedies, for in it the form is summed up and perfected. The different elements which characterize it appear in *Twelfth Night* in a more equal proportion than anywhere else: and they are more fully fused and assimilated to one another. As so often, it has its predecessor among Shakespeare's early plays. *As You Like It* descends from *Love's Labour's Lost*; *Twelfth Night* from *The Two Gentlemen of Verona*. The main motive of the romantic plot, the disguised girl wooing a lady on behalf of the man she herself is in love with, is the same in both. Moreover, it is a play of action as much as of talk: the plot is essential for the full expression of its central inspiration, and not just a framework and an excuse. Its source is less specific than that of *As You Like It*. There are two plots and they do not come from the same original. The original of the main one seems likely to have been a tale of Bandello. If so, Shakespeare has modified it a good deal. As usual, he has played down its more serious implications. These are slighter than in *The Merchant of Venice* or *Much Ado About Nothing*. Indeed, the only possible occasion for painful emotion is Viola's fear lest her brother should be drowned. Shakespeare makes very little of this. She mentions the fear; the Captain comforts her with reassuring hopes; Viola seems very ready to entertain them. Two or three scenes later, Sebastian does appear; so that the audience knows that Viola's fears are groundless, even though she does not. Thus we do not have much difficulty in accepting the improbable fairy-tale plot: it is continuously light and fanciful.

Besides, Shakespeare's characteristic lyrical comedy atmosphere is, as it were, richer and denser than elsewhere, subduing the whole play to its mood more irresistibly. Both the constituent elements of this atmosphere, humour and poetry, show themselves at their highest strength. *Twelfth Night* is at once the gayest and the tenderest of all the plays. There is no pretence that the story is likely. If we think it is as fanciful and irresponsible as a dream, so also do the characters themselves. Sebastian, the first day he arrived in Illyria, finds himself wooed by a beautiful lady of high rank he has never seen before, though she apparently knows him very well. He does not hesitate; bewildered but delighted, he accepts her kind offers. It is like a dream, he says, why not make the most of such a pleasing dream?

> What relish is in this? how runs the stream?
> Or I am mad, or else this is a dream:
> Let fancy still my sense in Lethe steep;
> If it be thus to dream, still let me sleep!

Orsino, learning that his page is really a charming young lady anxious to marry him, agrees to do so at once and gives up his claims to his old love without another thought. Illyria is clearly a place so happy and so wonderfully unlike any real place that, once we have breathed its intoxicating air, we are ready to believe that anything may happen there. For once Shakespeare has completely solved the problem of reconciling the claims of reality and imagination in such a way as consistently to create the impression which he wished lyrical comedy to make on his audience.

He solves its other problems too. That of structure, for instance: he has two plots, with the advantages of variety which that gives him. And he dovetails them one into the other as neatly as in *The Merchant of Venice*. According to his customary formula, he makes them run parallel till the fourth act when they come together in the duel scene. But he uses the device of the two plots to achieve a richer variety of tone than in *The Merchant of Venice*. There, both plots were relatively serious, though the Shylock plot was more dramatic and realistic. Here, Shakespeare elaborates the farcical low comedy elements in his entertainment, up till then confined to incidental scenes of clowning, and then turns them into the subplot. This has the advantage of balancing the farcical and the poetic elements in the play more symmetrically. The farce is not just an extra and extraneous bout of fun, it is of the substance of the whole composition. The parts are more closely and intrinsically related to the whole.

This is also true of the musical element, which so far from being a mere pleasing interlude, saturates the whole fabric. For the first time the play opens with a strain of music and ends with a song; and the two songs that occur during the play, like those in *As You Like It,* concentrate into themselves the pervading sentiment of the drama.

The characters, too, are subdued to the whole as much as in *A Midsummer-Night's Dream.* This is the more remarkable because they are more solid than those of *A Midsummer-Night's Dream.* Within their convention, they are as living as those of the other comedies. But each is kept strictly within the lyrical comedy convention. Nor is any dominant, even there. Even the enchanting Viola is not pre-eminent over her fellows as Rosalind is. And there is no Shylock or Don John in the play to add an incongruous note of blackness to the composition. No one in *Twelfth Night* is guilty of worse than folly. Thus, all the typical elements of the genre are present in *Twelfth Night*: the fairy-tale plot, the romantic aristocratic setting and characters, the broad English farce, the wit, the poetry, the music, the love motive. But they are better balanced, and the story is so contrived as to give us no difficulty in accepting them in an appropriate mood. In *As You Like It,* Shakespeare integrates his comic entertainment spiritually by relating its elements to underlying motives and ideas. So he does in *Twelfth Night.* The main motive is, as always, the love motive. As much as in *Much Ado About Nothing* or *As You Like It, Twelfth Night* displays the comic pleasing aspects of the most comic and pleasing of all passions. But with a slightly different slant: in *Twelfth Night,* he relates it to that sense of the incurable chanciness of life which is so important an element of his comic vision. Man is exhibited as the creature of changing and unpredictable circumstances created by the capricious god of love. Pierced by his sudden arrow, man finds himself in all manner of ridiculous, unexpected, and difficult situations. But there is nothing to be done about it. Chance and love are not to be resisted.

Both plots illustrate this thesis. The Duke thinks he loves Olivia, but fortune has designed that at the last minute he should discover that Viola is to be his bride. Olivia thinks of herself as grief-stricken for her brother's death. But one glance at Viola and she is head over ears in love with her, only to find a day or two later that Viola is a girl and that she herself is equally happy with Sebastian. In the farcical plot, the same theme repeats itself. Malvolio, unattractive and elderly, daydreams of marrying his lovely young mistress; and is by indulgence in this daydream laid open to the mischievous practical joke of Maria. Like the Duke and Olivia, he is self-deceived by his vain and fanciful heart. As usual, only the heroine sees the world with clear eyes. Not that Viola herself is free from the rule of chance and Cupid. But she realizes her situation and, with rueful irony, accepts it: "It is too hard a knot for me to untie!"

Olivia, though with less understanding of the implications of her thought, also recognizes the power of fate:

> I do I know not what, and fear to find
> Mine eye too great a flatterer for my mind.
> Fate, show thy force: ourselves we do not owe;
> What is decreed must be, and be this so!

And so, in fact, does Malvolio: "It is but fortune. All is fortune," he cries. He little knows how true his words are or how distressing his fortune is going to prove to him.

Thus, both in structure and in spirit, the play is admirably organized. It is worked out in detail with equal accomplishment. Except for the secondary character of Sebastian, there are no puppets in the cast, no characters without individuality who are there only too clearly to operate the machinery of the action. The Duke is not an impersonal, insipid *jeune premier* like Bassanio or Orlando. He is a subtle, ironical portrait of the aesthetic sentimentalist, a light comedy cousin of Richard II. He is not drawn unsympathetically, he reveals himself as possessed of all that superior sensibility to which he lays claim.

> If music be the food of love, play on;
> Give me excess of it, that, surfeiting,
> The appetite may sicken, and so die.
> That strain again! it had a dying fall:

O! it came o'er my ear like the sweet sound
That breathes upon a bank of violets,
Stealing and giving odour. Enough! no more:
'Tis not so sweet now as it was before.

How perfectly the charm and the limitation of the aesthetic point of view is summed up in this speech:

Enough! no more:
'Tis not so sweet now as it was before.

This is always the trouble of living for exquisite sensations! The outline of Orsino's capricious whimsicality stands out all the more sharply when we see him through the satirical eyes of Feste. "Now melancholy god protect thee, and the tailor make thy doublet of changeable taffeta. For thy mind is a very opal!" How brilliantly appropriate the images are, for rightly, they are pleasing as well as satirical. Opals and taffeta are pretty things: so was the Duke's spirit a pretty thing, for all its folly. Shakespeare, as a poet should be, is wholly unsympathetic only to the ugly. Olivia is touched in with an equally certain hand, the capricious, spoilt, charming young lady of noble birth. For she is young; a fact we are apt to forget when we see the part played, as it so often is, by stately actresses no longer in their first youth. We forget that it really was written for a boy actor of fourteen or fifteen years old. As for Viola, she has been praised enough to need no words of mine. Only, it is to be noted that she is another variation on the regular Shakespearean comedy heroine type, warm, high-spirited, humorous, but with her own delicate flavour of pensiveness and pathos, so that her humour modulates to a playful bitter-sweet irony and her moments of poetry are tender.

The figures of the subplot are equally individual, equally memorable. The chief of them, Malvolio, may be thought an argument against the view that every character is in tune with the general harmony. Once again, actors have confused the issue. I have seen Malvolio played almost as a tragic figure, an austere, dignified gentleman brought to disgrace and ignominy; and appearing at the end horribly distressed like a man freed from a concentration camp. "I'll be revenged on the whole pack of you," he cries with bitter tragic passion as he rushes from the scene. It is an impressive conception. But it is not warranted by the text and, in fact, makes nonsense of the whole Malvolio story. There is nothing absurd in so stately a figure aspiring to Olivia's love, even if he be a steward. No—the real Malvolio is a spoilsport, a fussy, pompous upper servant forever meddling in and interfering with other people's fun. "I think he is a kind of Puritan," says Maria. It is a good enough description. Shakespeare was against Puritans, especially in Illyria, land of pleasure and laughter. "Dost thou think, because thou art virtuous, there shall be no more cakes and ale?" asks Sir Toby. Surely his author means us to echo his words. No doubt in modern life, to get a person confined as a lunatic by way of a practical joke would be unforgivably cruel, but Illyria is not the modern world. It is not a real world at all. Even the Elizabethans, tougher than we are, would not take such an event quite so lightly in real life. Olivia and the Duke are sorry for Malvolio. But obviously they do not think he is being deeply and irretrievably injured. "Go after him and entreat him to a peace," says the Duke after Malvolio's final exit. And we must suppose that peace will be easily procured. For Malvolio's last words are not meant to be said in tragic tones. He gobbles them out to himself as he flounces out in a petulant rage. For if this were not so, Orsino, Olivia, charming Viola herself, are behaving in an unforgivably heartless fashion and quite out of keeping with their characters as these have up till then showed themselves.

The trouble is caused by the fact that Shakespeare's imaginative sympathy is so much richer and subtler than that of his readers. Though he sees Malvolio as a figure of fun, he also realizes that he has his pathos. And he touches on it with his own exquisite certainty. But the sympathy he shows him is a smiling sympathy. It is neither painful to him, nor should it be productive of painful feelings in us. Malvolio is a figure in Shakespeare's lyrical comedy world where neither bones nor hearts are broken. And he is rightly considered a figure of fun because he spoils other people's pleasure. He is not sensible: he is presumptuous and self-important and self-deceived. It is always the characteristic of Shakespeare's dream world that it is, paradoxically, the home of common sense.

Sir Andrew has his pathos too. "I was adored once," he says, anxious not to be considered out of things. In him we see an example of Shakespeare's power to transfigure a conventional type. The foolish, cowardly fop is a typical figure of Elizabethan humour. But Sir Andrew's particular brand of silliness makes him unique. Never has mental vacancy been more wonderfully expressed. He hardly understands a word that is said to him. When Maria calls Malvolio a Puritan—"Oh," said Sir Andrew, "if I thought that, I'd beat him like a dog!" "What, for being a puritan? thy exquisite reason, dear knight?" says

Sir Toby. Sir Andrew confusedly feels that he has missed the point but wishes to keep his end up all the same. "I have no exquisite reason for't, but I have reason good enough," he remarks with flustered defiance.

How different is all this from the satirical figures of Ben Jonson! Ben Jonson mocks in order to reform, or at any rate to punish. Shakespeare wishes to do neither. He does not sentimentalize Sir Andrew: he gives him no lovable qualities, to compensate for his folly. But he delights in his folly as part of the fun of life: and he feels that to reform him would be to lose some of this fun.

Shakespeare's own mood is best expressed in Feste, the fool. The fool in Shakespeare always stands a little outside the framework of the play, interpreting it to the audience by direct comment. He is in some sort a symbolic figure, at once bigger and flatter than life. We see this tragically exhibited by the fool in *King Lear* and comically by Feste. It is noteworthy that it is Feste who speaks judgment on Malvolio. Malvolio has rebuked him at the beginning as Puritans always rebuke idle gaiety. As he leaves at the end discredited, Feste repeats to him with delight his own words:

Why, "some are born great, some achieve greatness, and some have greatness thrown upon them." I was one, sir, in this interlude; one Sir Topas, sir; but that's all one. "By the Lord, fool, I am not mad": But do you remember? "Madam, why laugh you at such a barren rascal? an you smile not, he's gagged":

This speech must not be imagined as spoken with fierceness. Feste's tones are rather those of mischievious delight. Almost, as he speaks, he turns an impish harlequin somersault.

He is a poet, too, if he wrote the words of his own songs, the typical poet of *Twelfth Night*; and *Twelfth Night* is, with *A Midsummer-Night's Dream*, first among Shakespeare's comedies for its poetry. This has not the elfin magic that flickered over the wood near Athens, but it shows warmer and more heartfelt; and through its throbbing sweetness steals an undertone of pathos as through no other of Shakespeare's comedies. The sweetness is in some sort a bittersweetness. This does not mean that it is out of key with the comedy mood like the Shylock scenes of *The Merchant of Venice*, for there is no question of anything tragic actually happening in the story. Viola may speak with poignant beauty of her sister who had died for love. But we know that she has no sister, that she is really speaking about herself, and that she is far from dead yet. No—it is rather that in *Twelfth Night*, more than in any other of Shakespeare's comedies, we see that the very intensity of his capacity for joy brings melancholy along with it, because it is accompanied inevitably by the realization of joy's frailty. In Feste's song during the romping drunken revel at Olivia's house, the deepest sentiment of the play is concentrated.

> What is love? 'tis not hereafter;
> Present mirth hath present laughter;
>   What's to come is still unsure:
> In delay there lies no plenty;
> Then come kiss me, sweet and twenty,
>   Youth 's a stuff will not endure.

The Illyrian scene opens and we are admitted to a wonderful region of careless pleasure where lovely ladies, and princely exquisites, and gallant disguised girls, and comical drunken knights, and pert maids and pompous

stewards move before us in a multicoloured leaping mas-
querade, with the jester in his motley piping to them.
The music waxes faster, the fun more furious, the dance
wilder and more intricate, till at last, after a final flying
climax, the figures bow and curtsy and take their leave.
All but one: the jester is left alone, to sing a song, before
he too says good-bye.

> When that I was and a little tiny boy,
>   With hey, ho, the wind and the rain;
> A foolish thing was but a toy,
>   For the rain it raineth every day.
>
> But when I came to man's estate,
>   With hey, ho, etc.
> 'Gainst knaves and thieves men shut their gate,
>   For the rain, etc.
>
> But when I came, alas! to wive,
>   With hey, ho, etc.
> By swaggering could I never thrive,
>   For the rain, etc.
>
> But when I came unto my beds,
>   With hey, ho, etc.
> With toss-pots still had drunken heads,
>   For the rain, etc.
>
> A great while ago the world begun,
>   With hey, ho, etc.
> But that's all one, our play is done,
>   And we'll strive to please you every day.

This little, shivering, penny-whistle song is not much
in itself: yet—coming where it does—it is a supreme

stroke of genius. For it reveals by contrast how fragile and fictitious is the world we have been watching. The jar of realization is not unbearably painful; the fool can still sing. But Viola and Orsino and Sir Toby are vanished and we must put on our hats and coats and go out into the humdrum, everyday world where foolish things are only toys, and men shut their gates against thieves and knaves, and the rain it raineth every day.

Thus, in a snatch of street song, Shakespeare says good-bye to us: and good-bye as well to the golden comedy of his summertime.

THE TRAGEDIES
OF JOHN FORD

"Let the priest in surplice white,
That defunctive music can,
Be the death-divining swan,
Lest the requiem lack his right."

—*Shakespeare*

THERE is something autumnal about Ford's art, something that portends the end of a phase and a tradition. Again and again we can trace in his work the influence of previous authors. Shakespeare for example: *Perkin Warbeck* derives from *Richard II* and *Henry IV*; *'Tis Pity She's a Whore* has something of *Othello* about it; *The Broken Heart* recalls *The Winter's Tale*. It also recalls the work of that author who himself learnt so much from Shakespeare's romances, John Fletcher. Fletcher tamed Elizabethan tragedy. In his hands it grew lucid and courtly; it also weakened and softened. Ford's plays have something of Fletcher's lucidity and courtliness, and though they cannot be called soft or weak, they lack the fierce vitality of Marlowe or Webster. But Webster and his fellow tragedians have also left their mark on Ford. *'Tis Pity She's a Whore* reveals a kindred taste for fantastic horror.

Yet, though Ford learnt much from his predecessors, the result is not like any of them. For every element in his work is tinged by the colour of his intensely individual personality. It is the sort of personality that is more likely to occur at the end of an epoch. Subtle, exquisite, and well mannered, it has also something languid and overdelicate about it; it exhales a faint sense of perversity and decay. Caroline, not flamboyant Elizabethan, its characters embody themselves before the mental eye like figures in a picture of Vandyke, in which, against some background of pillared portico and stormy sky, curled cavalier and court lady in gleaming satin dispose themselves pensively before us in attitudes of mannered grace.

Vandyke figures; but as if seen through the eyes of El Greco! Ford's picture is irradiated by a strange, pale, lurid light, the light of his tragic vision of experience. Here it is that his originality shows itself. For though the elements of his vision are like those in other Elizabethan tragedies, Ford sees them in a different perspective and one which alters their significance. The older Elizabethan tragedy is always moral. Macbeth or Flamineo or Vendice commits an act of sin which is the cause of the tragedy. All the chief characters are conceived in relation to this act of sin; they are on the side of good or on the side of evil. In Ford's plays, too, people commit sins which lead to catastrophe. But Ford seems uninterested in them considered as sins. The moral indication of an act is not the aspect of it which stirs his creative imagination. Even in *'Tis Pity She's a Whore* he hardly seems to blame Giovanni for his incestuous passion. It is represented as something fatal and irresistible, wrong in itself, no doubt, but for which he is hardly responsible. Again, the tragedy in *The Broken Heart* does ultimately arise from that strain of vanity and ambition in Ithocles which led him to prevent his sister's marriage. But this is not a very bad action: and, in fact, Ithocles is not a bad character. There are no really bad characters in *The Broken Heart* nor in *Perkin Warbeck*. Ford, unlike Shakespeare, Webster, and the rest, does not see evil and suffering as caused by a breach of the divine law.

Indeed his outlook is more pessimistic than theirs. For him the acts that make havoc of human happiness are less to be considered voluntary than the expression of impersonal, irresistible forces of which man is the helpless instrument. His tragic heroes, Giovanni, Ithocles, Orgilus, are the victims of some obsessing demonic passion, against which it is impossible that they should struggle, once it has chosen to take possession of them. This passion, though it may be perverted into hate if frustrated, is primarily and predominantly the passion of love. Sexual love is the motive force actuating Ford's tragic heroes. So also is it the force actuating Tourneur's Vendice and Webster's Brachiano; but again with the same difference. Tourneur and Webster conceive of love in moral terms. Either it is high, spiritual, and lawful, or low, animal, and illicit. Only in the second form is it a sin and the cause of tragedy. Not so with Ford. He conceives it in more romantic terms—almost like a French "romantic" of the nineteenth century—as a splendid and terrible power, in itself neither good nor bad, assaulting body and soul equally, knowing no law, fatal, irresistible, mysterious. There is something glorious and worshipful about it, it is "absolute sole lord of life and death"; it is also disruptive, remorseless, destructive. Perhaps in *'Tis Pity She's a Whore* its destructiveness may be connected with its sinfulness, though since the hero is represented as unable to resist it and also incapable of seeing it as sinful, we cannot feel him to be very wicked. In *The Broken Heart* Orgilus' love is in no way sinful in itself, but only turns to evil vindictiveness when it is thwarted of fulfillment. Moreover, the blameless Penthea and Calantha are brought to suffering equally with the blameworthy Orgilus.

No! Tragedy as presented by Ford is due not to willful sin on the part of human beings, but to the incursion of an irresistible passion which at once glorifies their existence and destroys it. They realize its destructive power. It is an outstanding characteristic of Ford's view of love that it is associated inextricably with death. In some strange mystical sense love implies death. The sinful, lawless lover, like Giovanni, accepts death as the inevitable result of his passion even though he may not repent of it. The virtuous lover, like Calantha, welcomes death as the consummation of love. Only in death is love perfected, only in death is love safe from the injuries of a wicked world. Nor to pessimistic Ford is death the horror, fitly symbolized by grinning skeleton and loathsome, gnawing worm, that it was to the tragedians of the previous generation. In his characteristic mood he always speaks of death as of something desirable, an image of peace, tranquillity, and safety.

> Minutes are numbered by the fall of sands,
> As by an hourglass; the span of time
> Doth waste us to our graves, and we look on it:
> An age of pleasures, revelled out, comes home
> At last, and ends in sorrow; but the life,
> Weary of riot, numbers every sand,
> Wailing in sighs, until the last drop down:
> So to conclude calamity in rest.

A profoundly melancholy view of human existence! But not an ignoble one. For the spirit in which Ford confronts it is not ignoble. For all that his interpretation of man's predicament is not a moral one, Ford has his morality. It shows itself in the attitude which he seems

to recommend people to adopt in the face of humanity's
dark destiny. As might be expected, this is not an active
attitude; since man is necessarily a helpless victim of fate,
active resistance would be futile. But he need not give in
and he should not complain. He can be faithful to Ford's
ideal of virtue; an ideal constructed to fit with his view
of the universe; passive, stoical, subjective, its highest
qualities courage, fidelity, self-control, and these to be
valued for their intrinsic beauty, not for their effective-
ness. An exquisite refinement of feeling marks Ford's
most beautiful characters; the refinement of feeling
which leads Penthea to feel herself guilty of spiritual
adultery because she is married, though it is through no
fault of her own, to a man she does not love. Nor, in her
view, can this stain be cleansed by her husband's death;
she tells her true lover that she will never marry him, even
were she a widow, for she is forever too much defiled to be
a fit wife for him. This refinement of feeling goes along
with an overriding sense of the value of decorum in the
highest sense of the word. The noble soul owes it to itself
always to act with dignity and restraint. Ford's heroes
and heroines meet death and disaster with the outward
serenity of French aristocrats on the way to the guillotine.
The heroic Calantha, who continues to dance, apparently
unmoved, as messenger after messenger whispers to her
news of disaster, expresses in an extreme form the ideal
to which they all aspire. Her last words:

> They are the silent griefs which cut the heartstrings.
> Let me die smiling.

might be the motto for all of them.
  Ithocles, murdered by his enemy Orgilus, just when his

highest hopes seem on the point of fruition, does not protest or lament, but at once accepts his death with a strange, marmoreal calm:

> The earnest of his wrongs to thy forced faith.
> Thoughts of ambition, or delicious banquet
> With beauty, youth, and love, together perish
> In my last breath, which on the sacred altar
> Of a long-looked-for peace—now—moves—to heaven.

And Orgilus in his turn, meets his death in the same spirit:

> So falls the standard
> Of my prerogative in being a creature!
> A mist hangs o'er mine eyes, the sun's bright splendour
> Is clouded in an everlasting shadow;
> Welcome, thou ice, that sitt'st about my heart
> No heat can ever thaw thee.

Even passion-tossed Giovanni grows more restrained in his last moments; and his unfortunate sister, murdered by him she loved best in the world, breathes out her life in a sigh of infinitely poignant understatement:

> Forgive in heaven and me my sins: farewell
> Brother unkind.

This is more touching than the stoical calm of the male characters. And, indeed, Ford's heroines, Anabella, Lady Catherine Gordon, Calantha, and above all Penthea, are his most sympathetic creations. The passive virtue which he admired exhibits itself more naturally and gracefully in women, forced as they are by circumstances to be

always in some sort the helpless creatures of their condition. Ford invests their stoicism with a glow of pathos
and tenderness which warms and sweetens it. Just because they are frailer, their courage moves the heart more
than does that of his heroes; Ford's heroines have a pathetic beauty like those of that other tragic pessimist,
Thomas Hardy.

Not that his heroes are unreal. Indeed two of them,
Orgilus and Giovanni, are the most subtle and vital of all
his creations. They are the same type; pale, sensitive,
introspective youths who have been forced out of the life
of secluded meditation to which they temperamentally
incline, by the force of a dominating passion. They are
obsessed characters, whose very intellectuality, driving
them remorselessly forward by a sort of logic of the passions, makes them fanatical. Once again, the refinement
of Ford's mind and sensibility colours his mode of
conceiving character. Feminine strength he can draw
convincingly; but not the more robust and active
strength of the male. The men he understands intimately
are complex and weak, driven only to take the initiative
by the force of their passions.

Such a view of life and character was not completely
suited to express itself in the Elizabethan convention of
drama. And, in fact, it is only in *The Broken Heart* that
he finds the appropriate form fully to express his imaginative vision. *Perkin Warbeck* is an admirably sustained
and consistent piece of work, but it does not offer scope
for the exhibition of his highest qualities. In form it is an
historical play like *Richard II*, though its effect is different, because Ford, unlike Shakespeare, took little interest
in the political implications of his theme. Perkin's story

is not seen in relation to any general idea about the nature of government: Ford has made use of a piece of history to write a romantic and personal tragedy. All the same, the historic nature of the story does condition and limit the personal tragedy. Incident and character alike are simple, normal, and objective. Ford cannot employ them to convey his deeper, more original broodings and conjectures on the nature of love and death. The play is noble and touching but it lacks intensity.

Nobody could say this about *'Tis Pity She's a Whore*. Indeed its finest scenes, above all the death scene of Anabella, throb with a white-hot passion that their author never achieved elsewhere. But the final impression that the play leaves on us is somehow unsatisfactory and even disagreeable. Once again he is writing in a mode that does not completely suit him. *'Tis Pity She's a Whore* is a violent, macabre tragedy of blood in the manner of *The Duchess of Malfy* or *The Revenger's Tragedy*. These plays achieve tragic greatness because the physical horrors in them are necessary for the expression of the author's vision of reality. Vendice caressing the skull of his beloved, the torture of the Duchess, justify themselves as unforgettably vivid symbols of the moral evil which Webster and Tourneur are concerned to portray. But Ford is without this perception of moral evil: so that with him physical horror is just horror for its own sake, a Grand Guignol device for stirring a morbid shudder of delighted disgust. As such, it is curiously repellent, especially when we find it alongside Ford's subtle, civilized analysis of passion. There is a cold perverse sensationalism in the scene in which Giovanni appears with Anabella's heart on a dagger, which is unforgivably ugly. Physical horror is only admissible in art when it is endowed with spiritual significance; and this has none.

Further, there is a moral confusion in Ford's view of his theme which involves his striking a false note in the heart of his harmony. The Friar says—and there is no reason to suppose that we are meant to disagree with his opinion—that incest is a horrible sin. But Ford's fundamental indifference to moral implications of this kind makes him unable to make us feel it as sinful. On the contrary, the passion of the lovers is presented, deliberately or not, as something glorious; and all the more so because it is unlawful. How magnificent thus to defy the laws of God and man! Ford seems to be infected with Byronism before his time. The result is to make him fall into a Byronic insincerity. He appears to be making use of a moral system for aesthetic purposes, to accept the idea of sin in order to endow his hero and heroine with the glamour of a splendid sinfulness.

In *The Broken Heart,* however, he has found a subject that suits him perfectly. The setting is formalized and remote; not historical Tudor England nor contemporary Italy, but a formalized, imaginative region called ancient Sparta but with no more relation to the real place of that name than has the Bohemia of *The Winter's Tale.* There, amid palace and temple, general, courtier, and princess go through a strange stately drama which fitly symbolizes Ford's deeper vision of reality. Before the curtain rises, a disastrous act has been committed. From resentment and ambition mixed, Ithocles, otherwise a noble character, has prevented the marriage of his sister Penthea with her true lover Orgilus and forced her into marrying the contemptible Bassanes. All is awry. Penthea feels herself incurably defiled. Bassanes, conscious that he has not got her heart, is possessed by an insane jealousy; Orgilus is obsessed by the desire for revenge. Ithocles returns from the war and, realizing the results of his act, is filled with unavailing remorse. He is himself in love with the princess Calantha and asks Penthea to act as his intermediary with her. Though she has it in her power to frustrate his love as he has frustrated hers, she agrees to undertake the task. Calantha returns his love. But now the tragic consequences of Ithocles' original act intervene to bring catastrophe. Penthea has rejected Orgilus' suggestion that she should be unfaithful to her husband. But the strain of her life is too great for her strength; she loses her wits and dies. Orgilus, deliberately and from a perverse sense of justice, kills Ithocles, and then, without protest, allows himself to be killed as a punishment.

In the last scenes of the play, Calantha takes the center of the stage. She is now queen and gathers all her subjects for a solemn ceremony at the temple, where the body of Ithocles lies in state. Serenely she gives directions as to how the country shall be governed after her death, places a ring on the dead finger of Ithocles in token that he is her husband, and then dies of a broken heart, to the music of a dirge:

> *Chor.*   Glories, pleasures, pomps, delights, and ease,
> Can but please
> The outward senses, when the mind
> Is or untroubled or by peace refined.
> *1st. Voice.*   Crowns may flourish and decay,
> Beauties shine, but fade away.
> *2nd. Voice.*   Youth may revel, yet it must
> Lie down in a bed of dust.

3 rd. Voice.   Earthly honours flow and waste,
              Time alone does change and last.
    Chor.   Sorrows mingled with contents prepare
              Rest for care;
              Love only reigns in death; though art
              Can find no comfort for a broken heart.

These lines seem to contain the moral of the play; they
are the essence of Ford's profoundly pessimistic philosophy.

"Love only reigns in death. . . ." It is odd that Ford
says this so categorically, for the particular catastrophe of
the story need not necessarily have been looked on as
inevitable. If Ithocles had not interfered in his sister's
marriage, there is no reason why all the characters should
not have consummated their love. Perhaps Ford did not
choose the plot that best illustrated his doctrine. All the
same, there is no doubt what this doctrine is. The over-
whelming final impression left on the mind is that individuals cannot be held responsible for the tragedy of life.
Rightly, they live for love, the crown and climax of all
human aspiration. But since human happiness is of its
essence imperfect and transitory, this love can never find
fulfillment in this world. There is no condition when the
mind can hope to be "or untroubled or by peace refined."

Earthly honours flow and waste,
Time alone doth change and last.

The conclusion is inevitable: "Love only reigns in death."
Calantha realizes this; indeed, in this last scene she
seems to assume a sort of superhuman stature, to speak at

once as the voice of truth and to take upon herself the burden of expiating in her death the ill which mortal flesh is heir to. Charles Lamb has been accused of absurd exaggeration when he says of this scene:

The expression of this transcendent scene almost bears us in imagination to Calvary and the Cross; and we seem to perceive some analogy between the scenical sufferings which we are here contemplating and the real agonies of that final completion to which we dare no more than hint a reference.

These are bold words; but in fact they show profound penetration. Lamb's words generally do. Certainly this scene has a religious element in it. Calantha does seem to stand in some sense for the divine virtue which accepts suffering as a sacrifice for the sins of the world.

This religious element in the moral idea behind the play shows itself also in the way Ford presents it. There was a ritualistic strain in his imagination. His most typical scenes are always conceived in formal, ceremonial mode, as little realistic as that of an eighteenth-century opera; the scene in *Perkin Warbeck* when Stanley, about to be executed, makes a cross on Clifford's face, or that in *'Tis Pity She's a Whore* when Giovanni and Anabella kneel down to make a formal vow of love to one another. It is here that we feel the influence of the Shakespearean romances. The temple scene at the end of *Pericles* and that when Hermione descends from the pedestal to slow music—surely these are the models which inspired Ford. Most of all did it inspire him in *The Broken Heart*. The great set pieces, Calantha's dance and her death in the temple, are his highest flights in this manner. But the whole mode in which the play is written is ritualistic. Orgilus' meeting with Penthea in the grove—they kneel to one another in this too—and Penthea's interview with Calantha are composed in a kind of antiphonal duet. Even the death scenes of Orgilus and Ithocles are ceremonious. The victim sits or stands dignified and impassive to receive the deliberate death blow of his executioner. Ford's use of song, too, intensifies the formal operatic atmosphere. In a high dramatic moment like the death of Penthea or Calantha, a chorus sings a solemn dirge into which is distilled the concentrated sentiment of the scene. And the individual character of Ford's blank verse, smooth, slow, and regular, with its formal, conventionalized images, enhances the same impression.

And what an unforgettable impression it is! Perhaps Ford's is not the highest tragedy, for it lacks both the moral force and the full-blooded human passion of Shakespeare and Webster; but it is endlessly fascinating in its mixture of intellectual subtlety with tense passion, of hieratic dignity with heart-rending pathos, above all in its beauty. No work in English is more intensely aesthetic in its inspiration than *The Broken Heart*. The very conception of the scenes is instinct with a sense of the beautiful; the chance meeting of the forlorn lovers in the shadowy grove, Calantha's tragic pavane, her slow death to music. These linger in the memory like the strains of some concert for voice and viols by Purcell.

And even more memorable than the design of the scenes is the language in which they are expressed. There is nothing in the whole range of England's magnificent literature more "beautiful" than Ford's blank verse, and nothing is the least like it. We must go over the channel to Racine to find a parallel to its blend of classical purity and poignant emotion. Compared with Marlowe's or Webster's, its conventional images and careful understatements might appear colourless; compared with Shakespeare's it might seem constricted, so slow is its flow. For though rhythm is a more important instrument in its effect than phrase, the rhythm is not swift or violently varied. But it is never monotonous, and its delicate intensification by speaking, significant pause, or by simple word twice repeated, makes it capable of every effect that Ford wishes to achieve.

> Parthenophil is lost, and I would see him;
> For he is like to something I remember
> A great while since, a long, long time ago.

> Sigh out a lamentable tale of things
> Done long ago, and ill done; and, when sighs
> Are wearied, piece up what remains behind
> With weeping eyes, and hearts that bleed to death.*

>   Glories
> Of human greatness are but pleasing dreams
> And shadows soon decaying: on the stage
> Of my mortality my youth hath acted
> Some scenes of vanity, drawn out at length
> By varied pleasures, sweetened in the mixture,
> But tragical in issue:

---

* These first two quotations are from *The Lover's Melancholy*, a tragi-comedy, and as such should not perhaps occur in an essay on Ford's tragedies. But they are so beautiful and so typical of his style at its best that I cannot forbear inserting them.

Kiss me. If ever after-times should hear
Of our fast-knit affections, though perhaps
The laws of conscience and of civil use
May justly blame us, yet when they but know
Our loves, that love will wipe away that rigour
Which would in other incests be abhorred.
Give me your hand: how sweetly life doth run
In these well-coloured veins! how constantly
These palms do promise health! but I could chide
With Nature for this cunning flattery.
Kiss me again: —forgive me.

That remedy
Must be a winding sheet, a fold of lead,
And some untrodden corner in the earth.

When we last gathered roses in the garden
I found my wits; but truly you lost yours.

The voice is never raised; but how it yearns and trembles
and reverberates with the strength of the emotion concentrated within it!

His verse is of Ford's very essence. Mr. Eliot, who does
not much admire him, speaks of it as of some extra gift
he possessed, beautiful but significant of nothing but
itself. Ford, in his opinion, was a man of shallow, superficial mind with a talent for achieving certain musical
effects of his own in blank verse. Surely this is a confused
judgment. A verse form is beautiful and moving because
it effectively conveys certain meanings. Ford's rhythms
move us because they are so truly the voice of his strange,
subtle, and tender spirit.

THE FORMS
OF ENGLISH FICTION

"Really, universally, relations stop nowhere,
and the exquisite problem of the artist is
eternally but to draw, by a geometry of his
own, the circle within which they shall
happily *appear* to do so."

—*Henry James*

"A NOVEL," declares the Oxford dictionary, "is a fictitious prose narrative of sufficient length to fill one or more volumes, portraying characters and actions representative of real life in continuous plot." A clumsy, wordy piece of English, but truth lies embedded in it. "A fictitious prose narrative . . . representative of real life"—here is the crucial determining point to be remembered. The novel differs from other fictions—epics, fantasies and so on—in that it purports to describe something that could possibly have happened.

This means that the novelist is faced with formal problems different from those that confront other kinds of storytellers. Not altogether: since he is an artist, his work should have the formal qualities common to all good works of art, unity, pattern, harmony. But it must also seem probable in the sense that other fictions need not; it must give an illusion of life as it is or has been lived in the actual world. To achieve both these objects at the same time is hard. Real life, as we know it, is not distinguished by unity, pattern, and harmony. On the contrary, it is a heterogeneous, disorderly, indeterminate affair, full of loose ends and false starts and irrelevant details. How is the novelist to reconcile these two claims, how keep the delicate balance between the demands of life and art? This is his central special problem as a craftsman. The history of the novel, considered as a form, is a history of successive attempts at a solution.

It can be done by using a conventional formula. This was the practice of most great writers during the first period of the novel's history. The formula was devised by Fielding. In *Tom Jones* he wanted to give a big panoramic picture of life, and to show what he conceived to be the dominant motive forces in human character as they manifested themselves in people of different ages, sexes, classes, occupations. Nobody had tried to do the same kind of thing before in fiction, so he had no precedent as to form. His first novel, *Joseph Andrews*, had been in the picaresque tradition, that is to say, it had been a series of disconnected adventures only held together by the fact that they all happen to Joseph, the hero of the book. For *Tom Jones* he felt the need of a more purposeful pattern. He had started his literary life as a writer of comedies and he therefore turned to comedy for a model. Comedy had got a formal convention: the plots revolved round a hero and heroine, young and amiable, who wished to be united but who were separated from one another, sometimes by circumstances, sometimes by a deliberate intrigue, engineered by an ill-willed person. In the end the untoward circumstances were altered, the ill-disposed person was discomfited, and the intrigue resolved itself in the union of the hero and heroine. Fielding took this formula and, as it were, loosened it, stretched it, and then used it to impose an order on the episodic confusion of the picaresque romance. Thus he achieved pattern, thus he integrated his panorama. It was a useful formula, for it was at once firm and elastic; and writers who liked working on a large scale were immediately attracted by it. Some of the greatest English novelists of the next few generations, Scott, Dickens, Trollope—to name no others—with individual modifications, employed the Fielding formula.

All the same, just because it was a formula, it did not provide a complete solution to the novelist's problem. Order was imposed on the material from without, not evolved from within; with the result that the author's inspiration and his form were often at odds with one another. There is no logical reason why a picture of medieval life, or of the troubles of the London poor, should be forced into the pattern of an English eighteenth-century comedy. All too often in these books are we aware that plot, intrigue, hero and heroine themselves, do not really interest the author, that they are mechanical contrivances constructed to set the story in motion, and that like other mechanical contrivances they are lifeless. The individual characters and scenes of *Martin Chuzzlewit* or *David Copperfield* are printed unforgettably on our memories, but we forget their plots within a day or two of closing the book. Scott said that *The Antiquary* was designed to give a picture of Scottish manners at the close of the eighteenth century, more especially among the peasantry; the hero and heroine, however, are conventional puppet figures of virtuous young lady and gentleman, not typical of eighteenth-century Scotland or, indeed, of anywhere but the boards of a provincial theater.

Again, the Fielding formula often results in the stress of the interest falling in a different place from the stress of the plot. The most vivid scenes are, as likely as not, of minor importance in furthering the action. We remember *Guy Mannering* for Dandy Dinmont and Meg Merrilees, yet the theme of the story is the changing fortunes of young Bertram. Sometimes the fact that the plot is not part of the primary inspiration of the book seduces the author into diverging from it. Thackeray and Trollope leave their heroes and heroines in a situation of uncomfortable suspense while they are exploring the possibilities opened up by some secondary comic character that has taken their fancy. Let the hero and heroine wait! The authors know and the reader knows that they are going to be brought together sooner or later. The fact is that unity of form and inspiration can never be achieved by formula; only by genuine and radical integration.

The consequence was that, in their formal aspect, books written in the Fielding formula were never complete successes. Scott and Dickens were writers of high genius, but neither of them ever wrote a perfect book. Richardson and Jane Austen, the most skillful craftsmen among our early novelists, did not follow the Fielding pattern. As a matter of fact it only prevailed up till the middle of the nineteenth century. George Eliot dethroned it. She set out to write novels too soberly realistic and too intellectual in subject matter to be accommodated in a form derived from artificial comedy. Bit by bit she discarded conventional hero and heroine, intrigue, happy ending, and all the rest of the Fielding conventions. After her time there was no dominant convention for the form of the novel. The author makes it whatever shape he thinks best suits his subject.

However, his basic problem still remains. He has to discover some means of imposing an orderly pattern on reality without making his picture of it unconvincing. Roughly speaking, there have been three or four main modes of doing this. The classical mode is pattern imposed by situation. Of course this was not a discovery of the nineteenth century, it was introduced into the English novel by Richardson before Fielding ever put pen to paper. Since then it has been employed by many famous names: Jane Austen, George Eliot, Henry James, and in our time by Elizabeth Bowen, E. M. Forster, and L. P. Hartley. According to this plan, the novelist starts with a situation which he then works out logically to its conclusion. This process of logical development determined the pattern of the plot. *Pamela,* the first example of it in our literature, provides a simple illustration. The situation is this: Pamela, a virtuous servant girl, is dishonourably pursued by her bachelor employer, Mr. B. Since she is virtuous, she resists him. He redoubles his efforts, she redoubles her resistance, till in the end she has persuaded him to offer her honourable marriage. The action is worked out step by step as the inevitable reaction of given characters to a given situation, and every secondary episode, every secondary character, has its place in furthering it.

Pattern by situation is much more likely to produce the perfect work of art than the Fielding formula. For in it character and action are genuinely integrated. All the same, it is no more foolproof than any other artistic device. A writer may use it and still fail to reconcile fact and pattern. Sometimes we feel the claims of the pattern too dominant. In order to make his action orderly, the author has made it improbable. George Eliot fails in this way sometimes; though a solid, conscientious craftsman, she lacked the finer sense of her art. In *Silas Marner,* for instance, she has to make Godfrey Cass's marriage unhappy, for it is essential to the moral pattern of her story that he should suffer for that infidelity to a former love in which his marriage had involved him. It should have been possible for her to do this by indicating some fundamental weakness in his nature which made him discontented whoever he married. What she does is to make his marriage childless and Cass unhappy because he wanted an heir. This is not convincing; it seems to suggest George Eliot believed fickle men to be less likely to beget children than faithful ones. We feel reality has been twisted in order to give her books a tidy moral pattern.

To take a more modern instance, Mr. Graham Greene's novel *The Heart of the Matter* is designed to show how its hero, Scobie, though a convinced and practicing Roman Catholic, is led by a perverse benevolence to commit a succession of mortal sins. In particular, he commits adultery with a girl, simply because he is sorry for her loneliness. The situation is described with all Mr. Greene's dramatic force and it raises an intriguing moral issue. The only trouble is, it is very hard to believe it ever happened. Why should Scobie or anyone else commit adultery purely out of kindness? If the scene was set in some mysterious and allegorical region, we might swallow the improbability; but placed as it is in a contemporary West Africa described with all Mr. Greene's vivid power of reporting, it strains our credulity beyond a point that it can bear.

The novel of situation also runs the risk of lifelessness. The pattern is there, neat and orderly, but only certain sections of it are, as it were, clothed in living flesh; against these sections the rest shows up by contrast as artificially constructed bone. This happens in *Pamela* itself. The heroine, although a calculating minx, is an extraordinarily vivid character. Equally real are her unctuous parents and some of the sinister subordinates that Mr. B. employs for her seduction. But Mr. B. himself never comes to life. He is just a wooden figure of an immoral gentleman necessary to set the action of the book in motion.

This is a crude example of imperfect vitalization. But more sophisticated artists are also capable of it. Conrad's *The Rescue* is a beautifully constructed work, an heroic tragedy in modern dress, worked out with masterly certainty and told with a noble eloquence. Why are we not moved by it as we are by *The Mayor of Casterbridge* or *Anna Karenina?* Because the characters—Lingard, laconic man of action torn between passion and honour, and Mrs. Travers, alluring, enigmatic figure of femininity—are taken not from life but from Conrad's much-used property box. The book pleases as a piece of literary skill, but does not deeply move as a picture of life.

A more modern variant of pattern imposed by situation is pattern imposed by theme. *To the Lighthouse* by Virginia Woolf cannot be said to develop a situation, but it has a dominant theme, the effect of the flight of time on a family and its circle of friends. The book starts with them in one mood, one group of relationships. After a lyrical passage of transition entitled "Time Passing," they are revealed twenty years later with moods and outlook modified: and every passage of the book is designed to illustrate how this happens. Again, Elizabeth Bowen's *The World of Love* has as theme the influence of the dead on the living, as exemplified in the case of a man killed in the First World War whose personality still affects the woman who had loved him, and their children. The working out of this influence gives the pattern to the novel. Pattern given by theme, like pattern given by situation, integrates the book. But the author who uses it runs the same risks. In these two examples, the authors avoid them. But in others, Virginia Woolf's *Mrs. Dalloway*, for instance, we do now and again get the feeling of contrivance. The characters seem only partially alive, for only those aspects of them that illustrate the theme are made clear to us: and that is not enough to make them solid three-dimensional figures.

Many novelists, however, are not primarily inspired by situation or theme, and so a strict form does not suit them. The novel of character comes under this heading. "What first inspired you to write the *Pickwick Papers*?" someone asked Dickens. "I thought of Mr. Pickwick," he replied. Many English novelists might have made similar replies; Defoe, Charlotte Brontë, Goldsmith, Meredith of *The Egoist*, Joyce Cary. These authors are portrait painters: their subject is an individual person. The novel of character does not involve so strict a form as those of situation and theme. Episode and secondary character do not have to fit so tightly and neatly into the over-all pattern. However, the component parts of the book must still be integrated; bound together by some underlying principle of unity. Character and incident ought to illuminate by contrast or by similarity some aspect of the hero. Each should be, as it were, a branch or leaf springing from the central trunk of his personality and drawing thence its life. Once again the problem of reconciling pattern and reality presents itself. But whereas in

the novel of situation, reality is all too often sacrificed to
pattern, in the novel of character it is pattern that tends
to go to the wall. At its worst, the novel of character is
simply disjoined. In the first half of *Villette* Dr. John is
the hero, in the second, Paul Emmanuel. The only connection between the two parts is that Lucy Snow, the
heroine, is in love with each man in turn. Both phases of
her experience are enthralling, but neither throws light
on the other: the two sections of the book do not add up
to one whole.

Again, the novel of character can suffer from lack of
development. Even though the successive episodes need
not logically follow one from the other, each should contribute something new to the whole picture, either by
illustrating a change in the principal character or exhibiting a new side of it. *The Vicar of Wakefield* is an instance
of how to do this. We learn in turn to smile at Dr. Primrose in prosperity, sympathize with him in grief, and
admire him battling against calamity. Not so the heroes
of Defoe. By the time we have read a third of their histories we know pretty well what Moll Flanders and
Colonel Jack are like. We may enjoy following the rest
of their history because Defoe is such an excellent storyteller. But each episode leaves us with the same impression of the character when we have finished it as when
we started; with the result that our attention does begin
gradually to flag.

Akin to the novel of character is the novel of place or
period. Mrs. Gaskell's motive in writing *Cranford* is to
give us a picture of a particular kind of small-town society; Hardy writes *The Trumpet Major* in order to give
us a glimpse of life during the Napoleonic Wars. The

actions of these books are devised to give opportunity for these pictures, as the plot of *The Vicar of Wakefield* has been devised to illustrate the character of Dr. Primrose. In consequence, the novel of place or period, like the novel of character, has a loose form, and it is open to the same dangers. The string that unites the various episodes is liable to get slack. *The Trumpet Major,* for example, is conceived as a series of pictures exhibiting phases of life typical of Napoleonic Dorset; the arrival of the troops during an invasion scare when George III visits Weymouth, at the sailing of the *Victory* for Trafalgar, etc. These pictures are strung together on the thread provided by the love story of Anne and the Loveday brothers, soldier John and sailor Bob. It cannot be called a taut thread. In order to prolong the action sufficiently to include all the pictures, Hardy makes Anne waver now toward Bob, now toward John, now back to Bob again. With the result that though every part of the book is delightful, the effect of the whole is a trifle monotonous and indeterminate. Hardy has not completely succeeded in reconciling the claims of form and the claims of fact.

Indeed, not many novelists ever have. There are a few of them, however—Thackeray in *Vanity Fair,* for instance. At first sight the reader is hardly aware of its formal perfection. Thackeray just seems to have opened a window to show us the great flood of human life sweeping past spontaneously and irresistibly. But after finishing it the reader becomes aware that he is filled with that satisfying sense of harmony that can only be induced by a purposeful and integrated work. And, in fact, *Vanity Fair* is planned with a rigid and classical regularity. From start to finish it is designed to illustrate Thackeray's deepest conviction about human life: namely, that all men are more or less themselves deceived, and that the world is a Vanity Fair in every sense that the word "vanity" includes. In order to express its universal prevalence, Thackeray shows us it at work in the lives of two widely contrasted characters: Amelia Sedley, the gentle, passive lamb, deceived by her own weak sentimentality, and Becky Sharp, who plays upon the vanity of others for her own purpose, but is herself deceived by her own ambition. Further, in order to drive home the fact that the laws of Vanity Fair are universally at work, Thackeray introduces a host of secondary characters, most of whom are also conceived as contrasting pairs: George Osborne and Dobbin, the two brothers Crawley, Mr. Sedley and Mr. Osborne, etc. And all of these are represented as the victims of their own or other people's deception. And then at the close, when the curtain has fallen, the author steps forward openly to declare his moral to the audience. "Ah, vanitas, vanitatum! Which of us is happy in this world? Which one of us has his desire, or having it, is satisfied?" The theme of the whole huge work, implicit up to now, is at last stated openly. It is a wonderful technical achievement. Thackeray has imposed order on a huge and diverse mass of material; but the finished work is so pulsing with spontaneous vitality that we are hardly aware of his doing it. The characters seem to be working out their independent existence of their own free will, yet all their diverse histories combine together in a single picture of the nature of mankind.

More modest but more subtly perfect is Jane Austen's achievement in *Pride and Prejudice*. She had originally thought of calling it *First Impressions*; and the unreliability of such impressions is in fact the theme of the work. Darcy and Elizabeth Bennet, though in truth designed by nature for each other, do not realize it at their first meeting. On the contrary, she thinks him disagreeable because he has haughty manners; he imagines she must be vulgar because her mother and sisters are. The plot develops in such a way as to show how these mistaken first opinions are reversed; and the secondary characters and incidents each have a part to play in furthering the action. Elizabeth's sister, Lydia, is there both to exhibit the Bennet vulgarity at its worst, and to provide the crisis which brings Darcy and Elizabeth together; Elizabeth pays her visit to the Collinses at Hunsford in order that her creator might give her another chance of meeting Darcy. All is purposeful, all is necessary; but Jane Austen makes each character and episode so vividly real and so convincingly natural that the reader is even more unaware of her plan than when reading *Vanity Fair*: he just feels he is watching something happening in real life. Yet he is left with a sense of completeness and symmetry which, alas, real life seldom gives.

II

Reconciling fact and pattern is the first part of the novelist's problem, but it is not the only one or even the most important. A true work of art is more than just shapely. It must stir our interest and stimulate our imagination; it must be individual and significant and delightful. Here once more the novelist is faced by a problem that does not trouble other kinds of taletellers: for here again he has to concede much more to probability. The life we live in the ordinary world is far from being continuously significant and delightful. A great deal of experience strikes us as meaningless and trivial. How can the novelist convince us of the truth of his picture if it only represents real life as a life that is never meaningless or trivial? He does so by concentrating on those aspects of experience which are significant and delightful to him. His book must be less a picture of life than a picture of his vision of life, his interpretation of experience. This varies according to the bias of his temperament: it may be comic or tragic or romantic, or a blend of these and other moods. This means that he selects certain aspects of experience for his picture, and presents them in such a way as subtly to intensify them.

Art [says Thomas Hardy] is a changing of the actual proportions and order of things, so as to bring out more forcibly than might otherwise be done that feature in them which appeals most strongly to the idiosyncrasy of the artist ... As, in looking at a carpet, by following one colour a certain pattern is suggested, by following another colour, another: so in life, the seer should watch that pattern among general things which his idiosyncrasy moves him to observe, and describe that alone.

But, once more, he must not do this in such a way as to destroy the illusion of possible reality; once more, he has to keep a balance between life and art. Very often he fails to do this. It may be that he is so frightened of seeming improbable that he does not select with sufficient vision. Arnold Bennett's *Clayhanger* trilogy is a mine of information about the life of industrial England in the late nineteenth century. But only intermittently does it give us the sense of a work of art: for Bennett has not discriminated sufficiently between what is significant and what is not among the many facts at his disposal. The result is a photograph rather than a picture.

Trollope is another writer who tends to sacrifice art to fact. In his case it is not so much that he fails to select as that he fails to intensify. The secondary plots in *Can You Forgive Her?* or *The American Senator* are admirably true to life, nor are they weighed down by factual description in the way that *Clayhanger* is. The trouble about them is that they are insufficiently vitalized by their author's imagination. They are true to life and as dull as life.

However, great writers rarely sacrifice art to fact: their imaginations are too dominating for that. More often their books are vivid and individual but improbable. How far they have to keep close to surface reality depends on the nature of their inspiration. Jane Austen had to keep very close indeed, for her aim is to reveal the comedy implicit in normal life sedulously if she is to do this: she must persuade us that she is describing typical talk in a typical drawing room. If her subject had been some inner spiritual drama, she would not have had to bother so much about surface illusion. On the contrary, inner spiritual drama can only be conveyed in a mode that involves some degree of stylization. To quote Hardy again:

Art is a disproportioning [i.e., distorting, throwing out of proportion] of realities, and to show more clearly the features that matter in those realities which, if merely copied, might possibly be observed, but would more probably be overlooked. Such an artist needed a convention that gave scope for the expression of the spiritual elements in experience but eliminates the necessity for describing in detail its superficial appearance.

Hardy, of course, is thinking of himself; he was such an artist. So also were Hawthorne and Emily Brontë and D. H. Lawrence. But even these authors cannot afford to neglect surface reality to the extent that a poet does. They must not carry their stylization to a point where it clashes outrageously with probability. In fact, some of them do. Consider Hardy's use of chance. Chance formed a necessary part of his picture of the world because he conceived of life as a battle to the death between man and Fate, and Fate's actions, since they cannot be predicted, must appear in the guise of chance events. At his best they do so with extraordinary effect. That Mrs. Yeobright should arrive on her visit of forgiveness to Clem at the wrong moment gives the reader an extraordinary sense of the malignant destiny that mysteriously rules the lives of the characters in *The Return of the Native*. Hardy does not communicate such a sense when the hero in *A Pair of Blue Eyes*, also bound on a visit of reconciliation to his love, finds himself in the same train as is bringing down her coffin. The book seems not a picture of life but a pessimist's extravagant allegorical fable.

Similarly in Hawthorne's *The House of the Seven Gables*, the romantic shabbiness of the house does brilliantly image the fallen fortunes of its owners, the Pyncheon family. But when Hawthorne takes us out of the house and into the garden to show us that the trees and the flowers and even the chickens scratching in the dust are

also unusually sickly and shabby, our spirit of disbelief
wakes up and starts resentfully to grumble. We cease to
believe in the House of Seven Gables as a real structure of
bricks and mortar in a real New England street; it has
turned into an allegorical residence like the House of
Pride in *The Faerie Queene*.

Some novelists also err because they do not preserve a
uniform convention all through a book. Scenes and characters drawn realistically are interspersed with scenes and
characters drawn in a stylized convention adopted to
bring out their symbolical significance. The result is that
the book does not hang together. Consider D. H. Lawrence's story *The Virgin and the Gipsy*. Ostensibly it is
a realistic contemporary tale of a clergyman's daughter,
Yvette Saywell, living in a conventional family, and her
brief passionate relationship with a nameless gipsy passing
through the district. This fable is, however, a symbolic
representation of that clash between life-giving nature
and death-giving conventional society which was one of
Lawrence's obsessing preoccupations. The gipsy stands
for life-giving nature; the Saywell family for oppressive
convention; Yvette, the heroine, for simple human nature
torn between them. The result is not completely convincing because Lawrence does not observe a consistent
convention. The Saywell family are recognizably realistic
English figures, but the gipsy is an animated poetic symbol, more relentlessly and picturesquely enigmatic than
any human being could ever be. He and the Saywells do
not inhabit the same universe, and straining to imagine
one which could include both, our belief in the story
breaks in two.

Dickens is another writer who sometimes mixes his

conventions with disastrous results. The cause of his error is different. It is not that he brings in improbabilities for symbolic reasons, but that he does not understand the nature of his own imaginative impulses. Dickens was a grotesque genius; he vitalizes in so far as he caricatures. The reader learns to accept caricature as the necessary convention of Dickens' art. But a convention must be consistent: you cannot bring a realistically drawn figure into one of Low's cartoons. This is just the kind of thing that Dickens is liable to do. Pecksniff is drawn in a grotesque convention; Martin Chuzzlewit himself in a convention of insipid reality. When we see them side by side it is hard to believe in either.

Virginia Woolf makes the same sort of mistake in *Mrs. Dalloway*. The book is conceived as an impressionistic picture of a day in Mrs. Dalloway's life as seen through the veil of her fluctuating moods; the characters who appear in it grow clear or dim, definite or blurred, according as she reacts to them. Then suddenly Hugh Whitbread is introduced, the crudely drawn satirical figure of a type of worldling especially disliked by Virginia Woolf. The changing opalescent mists of Mrs. Dalloway's moods suddenly blow away to reveal Whitbread standing wooden and crudely coloured under the harsh spotlight of his creator's hostility. The book breaks its own convention and loses reality.

Indeed, the claims of form and spirit are as hard to reconcile as the claims of form and fact. Yet it can be done. *Wuthering Heights* tells us a far odder story than *The Virgin and the Gipsy*; for its characters and incidents image those spiritual forces controlling the universe according to Emily Brontë's extraordinary and original conception of them. But we never question its probability, because Emily Brontë keeps the balance between reality and imagination so exactly. For all their weight of spiritual significance, her characters are never the typical figures of an allegory. Heathcliffe and Cathy are as tangibly and individually real as is the heath on which they walk. Moreover, since the book is set in the same key throughout, we are not conscious of a jar as the story modulates from the real to the symbolic. Emily Brontë further helps us to suspend our disbelief by the extreme artfulness of her design. It is important for us to start the book in the right spiritual focus and get up to the right spiritual intensity if we are to accept what follows. In order to ensure this, she boldly begins at the climax of the book's action with the stranger, Lockwood, arriving at Wuthering Heights to find it the center of a thundering storm of warring passions and haunted by the ghost of Cathy. This puts us at once on the right imaginative plane for the rest of the book. We have, as it were, to start off believing in the supernatural, so that when Heathcliffe dies of starvation because he will not take his eyes off Cathy's ghost, we accept it. If Emily Brontë had begun the book soberly and tried to work us gradually up to believe in such an event, our imagination would simply have ceased to follow her.

Jane Austen's triumph is of a different kind. She is a comic genius of normal life. Her problem is to give us a picture that strikes us as typical of everyday reality, but which is also—unlike everyday reality—consistently amusing. A high degree of intensification will destroy the illusion of reality: Jane Austen has to depend rather on selection. As far as possible she excludes from her picture such aspects of reality as are not susceptible to comic treatment. There are no lyrical outbursts in her books, no important character dies, she never mentions the Battle of Waterloo. Her picture of life is always true to fact, but to those facts only at which a reasonable being can be expected to smile. She is careful also to survey her subject matter from an angle in which its comic aspects are most prominently visible.

Sir Walter Elliot, of Kellynch-hall, in Somersetshire, was a man who, for his own amusement, never took up any book but the Baronetage; there he found occupation for an idle hour, and consolation in a distressed one; there his faculties were roused into admiration and respect, by contemplating the limited remnant of the earliest patents; there any unwelcome sensations, arising from domestic affairs, changed naturally into pity and contempt, as he turned over the almost endless creations of the last century—and there, if every other leaf were powerless, he could read his own history with an interest which never failed——

Sir Walter's faults of character were grave enough to be described with complete seriousness. Jane Austen, however, concentrates on their absurdity and folly. It will be seen too that she induces the comic mood by her manner of writing. The light, lively rhythms of this passage, its sharp antitheses, are the expression of her prevailing spirit of irony. Always her tone of voice betrays she is amused. As she has reconciled the claims of reality and pattern, so she reconciles those of reality with the claims of her comic vision.

Once more I find myself praising Jane Austen. Not

reluctantly: I am always ready to praise Jane Austen. Moreover, to do so is inevitable when discussing the novel's form: for she grasped the laws governing that form more firmly than any other of our novelists. All the same, I would not be thought to suggest that formal perfection is the most important characteristic of a great novelist. Rather do we remember the great novels for their more creative qualities: for observation, for wisdom, for imaginative force. Even Jane Austen's own books live less by their shapeliness than by their acute insight into character, their exquisite sense of comedy; while some of the best novels ever written—*The Antiquary, David Copperfield, The Woodlanders*—are not shapely at all.

All the same, if they had been, they would have been better still.

SENSE AND SENSIBILITY

"Jane Austen was born before those bonds
which (we are told) protected woman from
truth, were burst by the Brontes or elaborately untied by George Eliot . . . . Jane
Austen may have been protected from
truth: but it was precious little of truth
that was protected from her."

—*G. K. Chesterton*

THE MOST illuminating comment on Jane Austen's work was made by herself. She refused to write the big novel of public life which some of her critics proposed to her; for, she said, it would be unwise for her to leave "her little bit (two inches wide) of ivory." In seven words, she reveals what it is that makes her the most consistently successful of English novelists. She realized her own limitations; and she had the strength of will to keep within them. These limitations were two in number, the length and breadth, as it were, of the bit of ivory.

The first was aesthetic, a question of form. She was a writer of high comedy. She approached the human nature which was her subject, from the satiric angle. And in consequence she deliberately excluded from her subject matter any theme or emotion that could ruffle the mood of smiling, intelligent detachment in which alone high comedy can be appreciated. She lived through the French War and the industrial revolution, but she never permits their shadow to darken the clear bright surface of her pages. There are no deaths in her books, no sublime speculations, no mysteries, no adventures, no crimes. "Let other pens dwell on guilt and misery," she said, "I quit such odious subjects as soon as I can."

The second limitation she imposed on herself arose from her social circumstances. No novelist, except a pure romancer, can write convincingly of worlds outside his own experience. Everyone remembers what disasters overtook Dickens when he left the middle and lower classes he knew so well, to describe Sir Mulberry Hawk and Lord Frederick Verisopht, or Henry James when he descended from the drawing room of the Princess Casamassima to grope delicately through the lurid dens of international anarchists. Now Jane Austen was born a woman, in an age when women were prevented by convention from mixing in any society but that they were born to; and the society she was born to, that of the lesser English gentry, was of all others that most ruled by convention. So that the world of her experience was necessarily a very small one. But she realized the danger of leaving it, and rigidly kept her stories to the world she knew. They all take place in England, all in her own period, all in her own class. Indeed she imposes further limitations on herself; and keeps carefully to her own age and sex. She never describes a conversation at which no woman was present, and never draws a full-length portrait of anyone but a woman of her own age.

Now any art so disciplined and vigilant cannot be perfected in a day. And for this reason *Sense and Sensibility* is not likely to be her best book. For it was her first. And as a matter of fact it is the most defective technically.

That sense of structure which was to impose on the seething chaos of the English novel of humour an order as lucid as that of a Greek vase, was an integral part of her creative inspiration; and showed itself in everything she wrote from the age of ten on. And the general scheme of *Sense and Sensibility* is as well ordered as those of her later novels. The theme is simple. Elinor and Marianne Dashwood are two sisters both charming, intelligent, and virtuous; but while Elinor's conduct is governed by settled principles drawn from reason and experience, Marianne trusts for guidance to the uninformed good impulses of her exuberant nature. Both fall in love, and both find themselves deceived by the object of their affections. But while Elinor's habit of self-control enables her to rise superior to her disappointment, Marianne collapses beneath hers entirely. In the end Elinor's lover, Edward Ferrars, proves guiltless, and she marries him; while Marianne, convinced by experience of her errors, is united to Colonel Brandon, an old admirer whom she is not in love with but whom reason tells her will make her an excellent husband. To this theme Jane Austen adheres faithfully. The story moves from Sussex to Devonshire, from Devonshire to London and Somerset, and a great many characters appear on the stage; but every character and every scene has its justification as contributing to the development of the main plot.

But though the general design is well enough, the execution is sometimes immature. For one thing, though all the incidents may play an essential part in the plot, they are occasionally ineffective in themselves, clumsy bits of machinery that do not well fulfill their function.

Edward Ferrars, for instance, has to be extracted from his entanglement with the vulgar Lucy Steele in order that he may be free to marry Elinor, but this should not have been done by marrying Lucy suddenly and unexpectedly to Edward's brother. Not only is it improbable in itself, it is too symmetrical; we feel we have left the realm of life for that of musical farce when all the characters on the stage are paired off in the last act. Again, it is, no doubt, essential that Marianne should learn some discreditable fact about the past of her false lover Willoughby after he has broken with her, in order that she may be convinced of his intrinsic worthlessness. But it should have been possible to effect this without lugging in that hoary piece of conventional melodrama, worn threadbare in a hundred eighteenth-century novels of sentiment, the seduction of Miss Williams, and the duel with Brandon. They are uninteresting in themselves; and they are wholly out of tune with the comedy mood in which the rest of the book is written. For a unique disastrous moment, Jane Austen has left her bit of ivory.

Finally, Marianne must clearly show her change of heart by marrying Colonel Brandon. But she should not marry him so soon. It throws doubt on the depth of her feeling for Willoughby. And if her feeling was not deep the whole force of the story's moral is lost. For she is then merely a sentimental girl whose attitude to life is the result of no genuine conviction; and there can thus be no interest in proving her attitude a mistaken one.

But these are incidental blemishes. Immaturity has betrayed Jane Austen into a more serious defect. One of the peculiar triumphs of her best work is that it so successfully satisfies the rival claims of life and art. She has designed it to form a logical whole as perfectly as if she were Henry James; but unlike Henry James, she has managed to invest character and event with such vitality that they appear as spontaneous and as uncalculated as if their author were Scott.

Now this is the result of a careful craft. The grooves in which the story is to run to its predestined conclusion are inexorably laid before she starts writing; but they are so hidden by the leaves and flowers of her fancy and observation that it appears to move with all the ignorant liberty of life. But when she wrote *Sense and Sensibility* she was not yet complete mistress of this craft. The structure is there, as we have seen. But it is not always hidden; the grooves sometimes show through. We are never for long unconscious of the author, moving the puppets, manufacturing the incidents.

It is partly that she enforces the moral too openly. If one is constantly informed of the lesson to be drawn from an event, one becomes conscious it is put there for a purpose; one does not accept it as an inevitable result of the situation. But it is due in an even greater degree to the fact that she does not bring some of the most important characters to life at all. Edward Ferrars and Colonel Brandon are ostensibly the heroes of the story. But from start to finish they remain as dead as doornails, lay figures of respectable men, provided for the purpose of marrying Elinor and Marianne at the end of the book.

Still more serious is her failure over Elinor. Here again the root conception of her character is excellent; shrewd, disinterested, calm-tempered, the perfect antidote to the undisciplined romanticism of Marianne. And now and again this conception is realized. "Oh," said Marianne, "with what transporting sensations have I formerly seen the autumn leaves fall. How have I delighted as I walked,

to see them driven in showers about me by the wind . . .
Now there is no one to regard them. They are seen only
as a niusance swept hastily off, and driven as much as
possible from the sight." "It is not every one," said Elinor,
"who has your passion for dead leaves."

In this one sentence are made to live for us all the
humour and good temper and common sense that should
be Elinor's. But, as a rule, Jane Austen is not content to
let her character reveal itself thus in word and action.
She has not yet acquired the art to show Elinor's virtues
silently, by a thousand small touches of nature. She must
proclaim and enumerate them. And in consequence
Elinor is smothered beneath her creator's commendations.
She remains in the memory an aggregation of good qualities, not a living person. In art as in life, example is better
than precept.

All the same, in spite of these defects, the predominating impression left by *Sense and Sensibility* is not of
immaturity. Of one branch of her art, the purely humorous, Jane Austen shows herself already absolute mistress. She had learnt her trade writing squibs and skits;
and whatever hesitation she may betray in her serious
passages, when she comes to a comic one she tackles it
with the easy brilliance of complete confidence. Her
humour grew subtler, it was never more triumphantly
funny. Who that has ever read of him can forget John
Dashwood and his growing conviction that what his
father meant by his dying request to look after his wife
and daughters, was helping them to move their furniture;
or Mrs. Jennings tiptoeing away from the scene of Marianne's disappointed love, "as if she thought her young
friend's affliction could be increased by noise." Or Mrs.

Palmer always determined to think everything amusing—"Mr. Palmer is so droll," she says, "he is always out of humour"—or Miss Steele, gallantly persisting in her unavailing attempts to persuade Elinor to rally her about the Doctor, or Mr. Robert Ferrars or old Mrs. Ferrars or foolish, friendly Sir John Middleton.

And even more entertaining than any single character in the story is the manner of its telling, that characteristic Austenian irony, so exquisite, so good-tempered, so ruthless, whose pervading presence it is that so decisively distinguishes her books from those of Trollope and Mrs. Gaskell and the rest of the domestic novelists that follow her. Sometimes it merely colours a turn of phrase as when Elinor, anxious to talk to Lucy Steele without being overheard, is enabled to do it "under the powerful protection of a very magnificent concerto played by Marianne"; sometimes it blossoms out into a little digressive passage as when the Dashwoods pay their first visit to the Middletons. "On every formal visit a child ought to be of the party, by way of provision for discourse. In the present case it took ten minutes to determine whether the boy was more like his father or his mother, and in what particular he resembled either, for of course, everybody differed, and everybody was astonished at the opinions of the others." But it is never absent for more than a sentence. No aspect of the story, however solemn, is protected from it. We find it pressed beneath each page like some delicious astringent herb and the whole book is sharp with its scent.

But, though only the comic passages are written with the full accomplishment of her mature style, the serious are even more interesting. Already she shows her extraordinary grasp of the social scene. How subtly and precisely does she define and distinguish the individual characters and atmospheres of the three circles in which the people in the book group themselves, the circles of the Dashwoods, of the John Dashwoods, and of the Middletons. What penetrating understanding of English family life and its complications does she reveal in her account of the relations between the different branches of the Dashwood family and the Ferrars.

And already she shows that unerring eye for the essentials of character that enables her to make a human being come alive in a line of print. If the reader wants to know almost everything worth knowing about the Miss Steeles, the Miss Dashwoods, and Lady Middleton, let him turn to Chapter XXI and read the two or three pages that describe an uneventful morning visit to Barton Park. While in Marianne Dashwood Jane Austen demonstrates her capacity to draw a full-length portrait.

For whatever loss the book may sustain by the comparative failure of Elinor is more than balanced by the brilliant success of Marianne. She might so easily have been tiresome, a hysterical Lydia Languish, whose charm we do not feel, and with whose sorrows we do not sympathize. And on the other hand, it would have been easy to paint her in colours so glowing, that the reader was won over to her point of view, and ended up on the side of sensibility against sense; thus finding himself in opposition to the whole spirit of the book. But Jane Austen, and this perhaps is the most important consequence of the persistent irony of her attitude, avoids both dangers. As later in *Emma,* she manages to create a heroine whom we always like, and always feel to be in the wrong. Marianne is far and away the most remarkable person in the story, the most attractive, the most original, the most sensitive. But her virtues only serve to lead her farther astray, to blind her more fatally to the realities of her character and situation.

She has a further and a peculiar interest as Jane Austen's only study of youthful passion. In one aspect alone did *Sense and Sensibility* gain by the fact it was an early work. In her later books, except *Persuasion*, she adhered so rigidly to the comedy mood that she never portrays intense feeling at all. And indeed there have been critics, from Charlotte Brontë on, to say she was incapable of doing so.

It it true that she never depicts it directly, still less analyzes it. But this was of the nature of her art. Her interest was not in ideas or feelings for their own sake, but as they throw light on character. She was concerned to write not about anger or love but about angry or amorous people. And this she can do magnificently. There is no more convincing picture in English literature of a woman in love than Marianne. She does not subside into a conventional romantic figure like the heroines of Dickens or Scott in a similar condition. She remains Marianne; but Marianne transformed by an absorbing passion. By a thousand trifling words and acts, we are made aware how love dominates her every thought, colours her every mood, isolates her from those round her, of the ebb and flow of her emotion, from its radiant spring to its numbed and bitter end.

Yet even here Jane Austen never allows herself to be moved from her prevailing ironical attitude. She may understand Marianne's feelings, she does not sympathize with them. She has no respect for undisciplined passion; it seems to her dangerous, misleading, and ephemeral. For Marianne may suffer all the ardours and endurances of Iseult and Juliet: in the end she is happy enough married to Colonel Brandon, seven-and-thirty years of age and wearing a flannel waistcoat.

It is this lack of sympathy, surely, rather than any incapacity on Jane Austen's part that has provoked her enthusiastically minded critics. For after her time the romantic idea of love ruled in fiction, only to be shaken in the last few years. Till then to speak unsympathetically of the heart and its yearnings was to take the Devil's side. Trollope was as level-headed a man as Jane Austen was a woman. But he was born two generations later; and the ideas amid which he was brought up made it unthinkable for him to represent a heroine as recovering from a disappointment in love. Johnny Eames was a more attractive suitor than Colonel Brandon. But Lily Dale lived single all her days.

And here we come to the supreme interest of *Sense and Sensibility*, its central thesis. Jane Austen has been criticized as trivial by the same enlightened race of critics as think her incapable of depicting passion. But such a criticism reveals a complete failure to grasp the convention within which her art is constructed. For aesthetic reasons she limits herself, as we have seen, to the mood of comedy and the world of the small gentry in England. But comedy can deal, and always has since the days of the Greeks, with themes as important and significant as those of tragedy: while the life of an English squire's wife is as serious as the life of anyone else: it can no more avoid the central problems that face mankind during its sojourn on this planet. The visible structure of Jane Austen's stories may be flimsy enough; but their foundations drive deep down into the basic principles of human conduct. On her bit of ivory she has engraved a criticism of life as serious and as considered as Tolstoy's.

And in none of her books is it stated more fully than in *Sense and Sensibility*. Its theme is akin to that of another early work, *Northanger Abbey*, but it is treated with far more seriousness. Jane Austen lived at a period of intellectual revolution. The standards of reason and common sense which had guided the larger part of educated opinion during the eighteenth century were being overthrown; and a new race of thinkers was rising who referred all their opinions to the guidance of the instinctive movements of the heart. On the revolutionary side were ranged almost all the distinguished writers of the day, Wordsworth, Coleridge, Shelley, Byron. Against them stood only one, Jane Austen. She did not most likely realize the significance of her position, still less her audacity in taking it up: for she lived far from the world of intellectual conflict and literary movements. But the fact is that in *Sense and Sensibility* this demure young lady was attempting nothing less than an attack on the fundamentals of the Romantic position. On the minute stage of her genteel comedy theater for the daughters of gentlemen, she presented the struggle that was rending intellectual Europe. Consciously or not, in Elinor is embodied the philosophy of Dr. Johnson, in Marianne the philosophy of Rousseau. And "Yes," Jane Austen seems to say, "yes, it is all very well to proclaim that passion and sensibility and a heart responsive to the beauties of nature and art are the only valuable things in life, the only trustworthy guides to conduct. But look how it works out in practice. Emotion uncontrolled by reason leads you into ludicrous mistakes, involves you in trouble that brings misery both to yourself and anyone you have to do with; and, in the end, it does not last."

It is beyond the scope of this essay to discuss whether she proves her case. But it could not be put with greater effect. And I, for one, am glad I do not have to answer it.

A NOTE ON
JANE AUSTEN'S SCENERY

"The most perfect artist among women."

—*Virginia Woolf*

THERE IS not much scenery in Jane Austen's stories. Her matter does not admit it. Novelists who make much of scene painting do so because the setting of their tale is an essential part of their theme. Either the action is connected with its setting or the setting is symbolic of the human drama. Hardy, for example, describes pastures and ploughland partly because he is writing about shepherds and farmers, and still more because landscape is an appropriate symbol for the impersonal forces of fate and nature, whose conflict with one another is his central subject; Egdon Heath incarnates that force of destiny against which its inhabitants are battling. Landscape is thus one of the most important characters in Hardy's books, and as such has a right to be described in detail. The ocean often plays a similar role in Conrad's work; the untamed Yorkshire moors of *Wuthering Heights* manifest that tameless element in the nature of things as Emily Brontë conceives it.

As with the works of nature, so with the works of man. In the books of Hawthorne and Henry James houses play the same part as moor and dale do in Emily Brontë's. The

Elizabethan manor house of Gardencourt, Madame de Vionnet's exquisite Parisian apartment, each in their different way stand for that European culture which is so fatally seductive to the American heroine and hero of *The Portrait of a Lady* and *The Ambassadors*. *The House of the Seven Gables* symbolizes the whole accumulated inherited past the Pyncheon family, molding the characters and conditioning the fortunes of its last representatives.

But Jane Austen was not concerned with the clash of civilizations or man's conflict with destiny. Neither are her characters shepherds or sea captains. She writes about the men and women of the leisured classes, in their family and social context; about Mrs. X's relations with her parents and children and friends and neighbours. Further, she surveys these relations mainly from the angle of satirical comedy. She is out to make us smile at human folly and inconsistency. Dramas of this kind do not require elaborate scenery. The satirical comedy of home and social life is too clear and extroverted to need expressing in terms of symbol. Description also is out of place in it. For visual descriptions relate to the sensual and imaginative; while satirical comedy, on the other hand, is concerned with ideas and moral qualities. It is intellectual. To interpolate much description into it disperses the comic atmosphere. In Jane Austen's dramas the characters are set firmly in the forefront of a scantily furnished stage. She realizes that it would be an artistic error to distract the audience's attention by filling up the background with conspicuous scenery.

All the same, her stage is not completely unfurnished. Nor is the furniture unimportant. For Jane Austen had a sharp eye for the look of things. She had an even sharper eye for the general effect she wanted to achieve. In her use of her descriptive powers she is, as so often, a model to other novelists. She employs them with great effect but strictly in the service of her main purpose. She concentrates our attention exclusively on those visual features which illustrate her human story and, for the most part, she keeps her descriptions in tune with the general comedy tone. Here is the Great House at Uppercross, home of Squire Musgrove, and Uppercross Cottage, the home of his son and daughter-in-law:

Uppercross was a moderate-sized village, which a few years back had been completely in the old English style; containing only two houses superior in appearance to those of the yeomen and labourers,—the mansion of the 'squire, with its high walls, great gates, and old trees, substantial and unmodernized—and the compact, tight parsonage, enclosed in its own neat garden, with a vine and a pear-tree trained round its casements; but upon the marriage of the young 'squire, it had received the improvement of a farm-house elevated into a cottage for his residence; and Uppercross Cottage, with its viranda, French windows, and other prettinesses, was quite as likely to catch the traveller's eyes, as the more consistent and considerable aspect and premises of the Great House, about a quarter of a mile farther on.

This is a clear, precise, recognizable piece of old England; but seen exclusively in terms of Jane Austen's human story. She confines herself to the scenic features that illustrate her characters: Uppercross is presented only in its relation to the life of the Musgrove family; the difference between the Great House and the Cottage is the difference between the old Musgroves and the young Musgroves. When she takes us inside these houses it is to exhibit these differences more fully. First Uppercross Cottage: "Mary Musgrove was now lying on a faded sofa of the pretty little drawing-room, the once elegant furniture of which had been gradually growing shabby, under the influence of four summers and two children." A brief sentence but a vivid one! We need know no more to visualize Mary Musgrove's drawing room. But once more it is presented in terms of her character and family life: the "faded" sofa, the "pretty" drawing room, "elegant furniture now grown shabby"; each epithet contributes to establish a picture of Mary's conventional feminine good taste, and also of her inability to control her children.

Equally revealing is the description of her mother-in-law's parlour:

To the Great House accordingly they went, to sit the full half hour in the old-fashioned square parlour, with a small carpet and shining floor, to which the present daughters of the house were gradually giving the proper air of confusion by a grand pianoforte and a harp, flowerstands and little tables placed in every direction. Oh, could the originals of the portraits against the wainscot, could the gentlemen in brown velvet and the ladies in blue satin have seen what was going on, have been conscious of such an overthrow of all order and neatness! The portraits themselves seemed to be staring in astonishment.

Jane Austen tells us enough for us to realize that the Great House was a picturesque old family place, marked at every turn by the traces of previous generations. A

writer like Sir Walter Scott, whose subject was man in
relation to his historic past, would have concentrated on
this. But Jane Austen does not: her subject was present-
day Musgroves. She says just so much about the past as is
needed to make us realize the present. The old-fashioned
room with its incongruous addition of new-fashioned
harp and piano and flower stand is an image of the family
life of the Musgroves; traditional but modified by the
activities of the younger generation in the shape of some
lively young daughters aspiring to up-to-date elegance.
Moreover, there is no question of Jane Austen exploiting
the antique in its romantic aspects. The old portraits
"staring with astonishment" are matter for a humorous
phrase, not a picturesque one. Jane Austen's manner
serves to maintain the key of comedy, as she also main-
tains it by the final caustic zeugma of the earlier passage:
"shabby, under the influence of four summers and two
children."

Compare her with a writer who is not a comedian: turn
from Mrs. Musgrove's drawing room to Mr. Rochester's.

A very pretty drawing-room, and within it a boudoir,
both spread with white carpets, on which seemed laid
brilliant garlands of flowers; both ceiled with snowy
mouldings of white grapes and vine leaves, beneath which
glowed in rich contrast crimson couches and ottomans;
while the ornaments on the pale Parian mantelpiece were
of sparkling Bohemian glass, ruby red; and between the
windows large mirrors repeated the general blending of
snow and fire.

This drawing room sounds as if it had been as typical
of its period as was Mrs. Musgrove's, and Charlotte Brontë
describes it quite as convincingly. But what a difference!
For it occurs not in a comedy but in a passionate love

story, and it is seen romantically through the eyes of the young Jane Eyre dazzled by the first drawing room she had ever seen in her life. How eloquently in character it is both with her feeling and that of the whole book that she should describe it as "blending snow and fire"!

Even if the Musgroves' scheme of decoration had also been red and white, such a phrase would have been wonderfully out of keeping in *Persuasion*. Indeed in her gravest moods Jane Austen is never unsmiling for very long. This is as true of her descriptive passages as of the rest of her work. Listen to her describing the old schoolroom at Mansfield Park whither Fanny Price would fly for comfort when unbearably oppressed by loneliness and lack of sympathy:

The room was most dear to her, and she would not have changed its furniture for the handsomest in the house, though what had been originally plain had suffered all the ill-usage of children; and its greatest elegancies and ornaments were a faded footstool of Julia's work, too ill done for the drawing-room, three transparencies, made in a rage for transparencies, for the three lower panes of one window, where Tintern Abbey held its station between a cave in Italy and a moonlight lake in Cumberland, a collection of family profiles, thought unworthy of being anywhere else, over the mantel-piece; and by their side, and pinned against the wall, a small sketch of a ship sent four years ago from the Mediterranean by William, with H.M.S. Antwerp at the bottom, in letters as tall as the mainmast.

Footstool "too ill done for the drawing-room"; the sketch of the Antwerp with "letters as tall as the mainmast"—

Jane Austen is still smiling: these phrases are touched with
her characteristic irony. But here it is softened to a tender
irony in harmony with her sympathy for the pathos of
Fanny's lot. On the other hand, the description contains
much more detail about the physical facts of the scene
than is common in Jane Austen's books. Rightly so; she
needs it to evoke and convey the heightened, intimate
intensity of Fanny's sentiment for the room.

Even more physical and more detailed is the account of
Fanny's squalid Portsmouth home on her first unhappy
evening there:

The sun's rays falling strongly into the parlour, instead
of cheering, made her still more melancholy; for sunshine
appeared to her a totally different thing in a town and in
the country. Here, its power was only a glare, a stifling,
sickly glare, serving but to bring forward stains and dirt
that might otherwise have slept. There was neither health
nor gaiety in sunshine in a town. She sat in a blaze of oppressive heat, in a cloud of moving dust; and her eyes
could only wander from the walls marked by her father's
head, to the table cut and knotched by her brothers, where
stood the tea-board never thoroughly cleaned, the cups
and saucers wiped in streaks, the milk a mixture of motes
floating in thin blue, and the bread and butter growing
every minute more greasy than even Rebecca's hands had
first produced it. Her father read his newspaper, and her
mother lamented over the ragged carpet as usual, while
the tea was in preparation.

This passage is the final answer to those who accuse
Jane Austen of shirking the ugly facts of life, of being
incurably genteel. She is only genteel in so far as she is

writing about genteel society. If her story takes her away
from it, she can describe the sordid as ruthlessly as anyone
and with as vivid an eye for the physical detail—the
grease-marked wall, the dirty milk. But she always remembers that a description is only significant if it illustrates the particular human drama which is her subject.
As a matter of fact her grip on character is so close that
the reader finds himself imagining the houses which she
does not describe—just because he knows so much about
the people who live in them. Obviously Mansfield Park
was well-appointed and dignified, Hartfield old-fashioned, unpretentious and comfortable—we remember
how much Mr. Woodhouse hated draughts—Kellynch
Hall stylish, but a touch showy.

It is Jane Austen's indoor settings that come to the
mind first, for in the main her stories take place indoors.
But her occasional landscapes are equally convincing.
In real life she took great pleasure in the spectacle of the
natural scene—was not Crabbe her favourite poet? She
also quotes Cowper. Her choice of these two writers is
characteristic. She loved nature in the eighteenth-
century manner; it is not to her, as it was to the romantics, the incarnation of some mysterious indwelling spirit,
but rather a pleasant background to life, softening the
heart and elevating the mind by its beauty and freshness
and peace.

Fanny agreed to it, and had the pleasure of seeing him
continue at the window with her, in spite of the expected
glee; and of having his eyes soon turned like her's towards
the scene without, where all that was solemn and soothing, and lovely, appeared in the brilliancy of an unclouded

night, and the contrast of the deep shade of the woods.
Fanny spoke her feelings. "Here's harmony!" said she,
"Here's repose! Here's what may leave all painting and
all music behind, and what poetry only can attempt to
describe. Here's what may tranquillize every care, and
lift the heart to rapture! When I look out on such a night
as this, I feel as if there could be neither wickedness nor
sorrow in the world; and there certainly would be less of
both if the sublimity of Nature were more attended to,
and people were carried more out of themselves by contemplating such a scene."

"I like to hear your enthusiasm, Fanny. It is a lovely
night, and they are much to be pitied who have not been
taught to feel in some degree as you do—who have not at
least been given a taste for nature in early life. They lose
a great deal."

"*You* taught me to think and feel on the subject,
cousin."

"I had a very apt scholar. There's Arcturus looking
very bright."

"Yes, and the bear. I wish I could see Cassiopeia."

"We must go out on the lawn for that. Should you be
afraid?"

"Not in the least. It is a great while since we have had
any star-gazing."

This is an extraordinary passage. How completely it
suggests the starry serenity of the summer night in contrast with the hot, candle-lit drawing room, tense with
frustrated conflicting emotions! Yet Jane Austen has
contrived to do this with a Racine-like economy of means.
There is one generalized descriptive phrase "the brilliancy
of an unclouded night, and the contrast of the deep shade
of the woods." Otherwise, the effect is conveyed solely by

the names of the constellations as Edmund and Fanny mention them in their talk. To have made these express themselves more eloquently would have been out of character with their sober English personalities. Coming where they do, however, these names, Arcturus and Cassiopeia—fraught as they are with poetical and mythological associations—are enough for Jane Austen's purpose. Finally, Fanny's little rhapsodical outburst keeps the scene related to the personal drama. Our eyes are directed to the night sky only because it symbolizes those purer, nobler aspirations felt by Fanny but unknown to the worldly Bertrams and Crawfords among whom she lives.

It is to be noted that there are no similar passages in *Pride and Prejudice* or *Emma*; partly because their heroines are not so poetically minded as Fanny, but also because the whole tone of these books is lighter. *Mansfield Park* is a comedy in the main, but its theme is not essentially a comic theme as those of the other two are, and its general tone is graver. Jane Austen, therefore, allows herself to strike a more lyrical note than would have been appropriate in *Pride and Prejudice*.

Yet more strongly does she sound it in *Persuasion*. Here the heroine, Anne Elliott, is also sad, lonely, and responsive to the soothing influences of nature, while the theme, faithful love, its nature and obligations, gives more scope for the romantic strain in Jane Austen's imagination than that of *Mansfield Park* does. As a result landscape plays a more important part in *Persuasion* than in any of her other books. As in no other we are aware of the country, the weather, the season. One scene especially comes to mind. Anne finds herself on a country walk in the same party in which her former lover Wentworth is flirting with another girl:

Her pleasure in the walk must arise from the exercise and the day, from the view of the last smiles of the year upon the tawny leaves and withered hedges, and from repeating to herself some few of the thousand poetical descriptions extant of autumn, that season of peculiar and inexhaustible influence on the mind of taste and tenderness, that season which has drawn from every poet, worthy of being read, some attempt at description, or some lines of feeling. She occupied her mind as much as possible in such like musings and quotations; but it was not possible, that when within reach of Captain Wentworth's conversation with either of the Miss Musgroves, she should not try to hear it; . . . There was one speech of Louisa's which struck her. After one of the many praises of the day, which were continually bursting forth, Captain Wentworth added, "What glorious weather for the Admiral and my sister! They meant to take a long drive this morning; perhaps we may hail them from some of these hills. They talked of coming into this side of the country. I wonder whereabouts they will upset to-day. Oh! it does happen very often, I assure you—but my sister makes nothing of it—she would as lieve be tossed out as not."

"Ah! You make the most of it, I know," cried Louisa, "but if it were really so, I should do just the same in her place. If I loved a man, as she loves the Admiral, I would be always with him, nothing should ever separate us, and I would rather be overturned by him, than driven safely by anybody else."

It was spoken with enthusiasm.

"Had you?" cried he, catching the same tone; "I honour you!" And there was silence between them for a little while.

Anne could not immediately fall into a quotation again. The sweet scenes of autumn were for a while put by—unless some tender sonnet, fraught with the apt analogy of the declining year, with declining happiness, and the images of youth and hope, and spring, all gone together, blessed her memory. She roused herself to say, as they struck by order into another path, "Is not this one of the ways to Winthrop?" But nobody heard, or, at least, nobody answered her.

. . . After another half mile of gradual ascent through large enclosures, where the ploughs at work, and the fresh-made path spoke the farmer, counteracting the sweets of poetical despondence, and meaning to have spring again, they gained the summit of the most considerable hill, which parted Uppercross and Winthrop, and soon commanded a full view of the latter, at the foot of the hill on the other side.

At first glance this seems to be in Jane Austen's customary manner. The descriptive touches are very slight, "tawny leaves," "withered hedgerows"; and she still takes care to preserve the comedy and common sense atmosphere by laughing at any extravagant indulgence in the "sweets of poetical despondence." All the same, landscape is playing a different and stronger role than in her earlier books. The pensive autumnal weather reflects the sentiment in the heart of the heroine; while the cheerful note of the last paragraph, "the ploughs at work, and the fresh-made path spoke the farmer, . . . meaning to have spring again," indicates that her future is more hopeful than she realizes. In fact, though shyly and with hesitation, Jane Austen is using landscape as Hardy and Emily Brontë did, not merely as a background but in order also to symbolize the emotions animating her human drama. It is the first time she has done so; and in her latest book. Would she have gone further on these lines, had she lived to write others? Here is another of the unknowable things about Jane Austen that one longs to know.

JOSEPH CONRAD

"To turn events into ideas is the
function of literature."

—*George Santayana*

I

CONRAD'S novels are like no one else's. How should they be, it may be asked, seeing that they are the work of a Pole nurtured on French and Russian novels, but writing in English? Besides, he was in himself a man of curiously blended disposition. There was the man-of-action strain in him first of all. By nature virile and adventurous, he was born, an aristocratic Pole, at a time when Poland was groaning under the tyranny of Russia, and grew up in an atmosphere of danger and desperate exploit, acquainted with heroes, on the one hand, and, on the other, with spies and informers. There was clearly no future for him in his own country; he therefore joined first the French and then the English Merchant Service, was involved for a time in gunrunning for the Carlists in the Mediterranean; and, before he finally settled down as an author, had sailed all over the world, notably to the Far East, still an untamed and mysterious region where every white man was a pioneer.

Most creative novelists draw their inspiration from that youthful period when their imagination was most intensely receptive. Conrad is no exception to this rule. His creative range is bounded by his experience before thirty. He never writes of a secure and civilized society. The conditions under which his characters live are pre-eminently lawless and primitive, in the wild East of those days, for instance, or the rough Merchant Service, where men have to prove themselves by the sheer strength of their personal qualities, unhelped by the force of any supporting social order; and where they are frequently in danger of death from man or savage nature. This is the setting of the early books of *Youth* and *Typhoon* and *The End of the Tether* and *Lord Jim*. Even when Conrad does go on shore it is to a world in which the safe order of life has been shattered by tyranny or revolution: or to that underworld of outcasts who are in arms against it. The Southern American Republic of *Nostromo* is rent asunder by brutal civil war; *Under Western Eyes* and *The Secret Agent* deal with nihilists and revolutionaries, seeking to destroy by violent means the existing social structure; his two historical novels *The Rover* and *Suspense* treat of a Europe split in sunder by the French Revolution and the Napoleonic wars; *The Arrow of Gold* recalls his Carlist experiences.

The characters, too, are in keeping with their setting, men of action and of violence, soldiers, sailors, criminal adventurers, revolutionaries. They are mostly men; Conrad's world is a masculine world. Such women as he does include are also for some reason or other outlaws. Donna Rita, Flora le Barral, Arlette, Lena—they are all waifs and strays, deprived of sheltering background, cast adrift by misfortune on the wild ocean of existence. And the stories, in which men and women alike are involved, are stories of adventure and danger and heroism and ruthless violence; full of fights and flights and suspense.

So far Conrad's books might seem to belong to the same type as Stevenson's. Yet they are profoundly different; for he regards his material from so different an angle of vision. Here we come to the second outstanding feature of his genius. His was a brooding, questioning intelligence, out to explore the motives behind the simple violent events he describes and to discover their universal application; so that though his plots may be like Stevenson's, their focus of interest is much more like Hardy's. The thrilling, highly coloured adventure tales are for him the vehicle through which he expresses his sense of man's predicament in the universe. His subject is not men but man; man face to face with his inescapable destiny of which this picturesque world of romance and action which he writes about is only one manifestation. Behind the stirring events, through the vivid, exotic scenery, are discernible the stern lines of Conrad's view of life.

It is a view of life, moreover, very unlike that of the average adventure-story writer: a complex mixture of pessimistic skepticism and romantic faith. The pessimism was the result of his experience; which had taught him that life was of its nature precarious, that security was a delusion only believed in by people fortunate enough not to have noticed the abyss of danger that yawned beneath that smooth frail surface of their existence, which could at any moment be shattered into fragments. There was no end, no limit to life's capacity for catastrophe and disaster. "Since the Day of Creation," he says, "two

veiled figures, Doubt and Melancholy, are pacing endlessly in the sunshine of the world."

You will note that doubt accompanies melancholy.
The second effect of his early experience was to leave
him with a deep distrust of those official faiths and ideals
with the help of which human beings try to fortify themselves against the despair engendered by life's tragic inse-
curity, the lights by which they strive to guide themselves
through its chaotic darkness. What Conrad had seen of
the world had convinced him that they were illusions—
often dangerous illusions—founded on nothing firmer
than hope, vanity, and ignorance. So far from being
guiding lights of truth, they were will-o'-the-wisps, the
pursuit of which was only too likely to plunge man
deeper and more disastrously into chaos. A childhood
spent amid the follies and futilities of political struggle
had left him unable to take sides. Were not the supporters
of both parties in these struggles always and equally biased
and corrupted by their beliefs? Were not these beliefs
equally figments and dreams conjured up by man to hide
from himself the sad inexplicability of his condition?
For this reason Conrad particularly detested revolutionary enthusiasm. "Its hard absolute optimism," he says,
"is repulsive by the menace of fanaticism and intolerance
it contains." A faith in an ancient tradition was less
unsympathetic; that at least was rooted in some experience of reality. But even for this his sympathy was
qualified. *Suspense* shows him more friendly to the gen-
erous, reckless followers of the Napoleonic dream than to
the cynical, dry-hearted supporters of the old regime. A
spirit so disenchanted with this world often turns in hope
to the other, but Conrad, though in no sense a materialist,

was apparently without the religious instinct. For him, as to the pagans of the ancient North, man's life was a flicker of light in an unfathomable darkness. The world was a place of tragic mystery through which bewildered man, blinded by illusion and vanity, struggled his aimless way till death came to consign him to the nothingness from which he had come.

All the same—and this is what gives its distinctive individuality to his point of view—Conrad was not a complete skeptic. For he never felt life to be worthless. It was enigmatic and terrible; it was also enthralling and splendid and beautiful; a magnificent spectacle stirring the heart, uplifting the imagination, one could not tell why. And man—deluded man—he could be a noble spectacle too, with his huge potentialities for love and admiration and courage and self-sacrifice. Even if most causes were valueless, the individuals who fought for them were not. Even if the object to which man devoted himself were nonexistent, that did not make the grandeur of his devotion to it less, nor destroy the value of the spirit in which he pursued it. What one lives for may be uncertain, how one lives is not. This instinctive response to life gives Conrad a faith and a morality. Man should live nobly though he does not see any practical reason for it, simply because in the mysterious inexplicable mixture of beauty and ugliness, virtue and baseness in which he finds himself he must want to be on the side of the beautiful and the virtuous. As a writer instinctively wants to express himself in the best style he can, so a man must want to live in the best style he can, to make his character as like as possible to the things in his experience which call out his admiration and sense of glory.

"I wondered," says the hero of *The Secret Sharer*, "how far I should turn out faithful to that ideal of one's own personality every man sets up for himself secretly." So might all of his heroes have spoken, so might Conrad have spoken himself. To him the final betrayal was to allow oneself to be cowed by the danger and disaster of existence into surrendering that faith in the value of individual nobility which is implanted in the human soul at birth. In the light of this conviction human beings, as Conrad sees them, divide themselves into two moral categories: those who hold fast to their faith in their personal ideal of virtue and determine their actions in reference to it, on the one hand; and, on the other, those who from weakness or blindness are false to it. "All men," he said, "must choose to sacrifice their Gods to their passions or their passions to their Gods." Life, in his view, is a moral drama in which the conflict turns on how far or not human beings can succeed in living up to their innate vision of virtue.

This vision is what one might expect from someone of his temperament and experience. It is a militant ideal. Conrad admires those virtues which count most in a life of danger and action; the virtues of the soldier at his post and the steersman at the helm. Courage, loyalty, fidelity, tenacity—experience had taught him that without these man was helpless and worthless when it came to the test of action. At the same time, Conrad was skeptical of the value of action in itself. He admired practical virtues for their ideal beauty; and he conceived them in a much more elevated way than commonly. He praises Henry James as "the historian of fine consciences." But so equally was he. It is the precise quality of fidelity, loyalty, and so on, that he is out to discriminate. Only at its finest does it win his full approval. His moral sense is further civilized by tradition. His ideal hero was a knightly hero who besides being brave and loyal was dignified, chivalrous, compassionate, and vowed to the service of a rigid standard of personal conduct, the slightest violation of which is an unappeasable torment to his conscience. It is a stain on his inner ideal of himself, his honour; and the conception of personal honour is the center of Conrad's moral system. The man who preserves it is saved, the man who loses it is damned.

The Frenchman in Lord Jim says,

"The honour, Monsieur, that is real. And what life may be worth when the honour is gone—I can offer no opinions. . . ."

"Very well," I said with a disconcerted smile, "but couldn't it reduce itself to not being found out?"

"This Monsieur is too fine for me," he replied.

The Frenchman speaks ironically; this final and absolute insistence on the obligations of honour is to him the distinguishing mark of the highest virtue. So it is to his creator.

This is the heroic ideal: it is also an aristocratic ideal. Conrad was not in the least a snob. The characters he creates for our highest admiration—Captain Whalley and Captain McWhirr, Viola the innkeeper, old Singleton the common sailor—are of humble birth and little education. But they are exceptional men. And Conrad takes for granted that the highest virtue is the exclusive possession of exceptional man. He has no democratic enthusiasm for the homely virtues of the average person. Life was too stern a struggle in too unfriendly a universe for these to be of much avail. He looks on average mankind with a stately contemptuous pity. Admiration was due only to the few, the heroes: for the most part obscure, unadmired, unrewarded, but in fact the only true masters of their fate and captains of their souls.

Aristocratic too is the emphasis Conrad lays on style, on "manner" in the broadest sense. "*Il y a toujours la manière,*" he quotes. "Very true. Yes. There is the manner. The manner in laughter, in tears, in irony, in indignations and enthusiasms, in judgements—even in love." All Conrad's admirable characters feel this. Even humble sailors like Nostromo and Captain Whalley care for appearances; they wish to present themselves to the world in accordance with some ideal of demeanour. If they are English it is a plain and reticent ideal; more typically it is Continental, an elaborate grand-seigneur affair, at once ceremonious and aloof.

Conrad's humanity, then, divides itself into two categories, those who try to adhere to their inner ideal of virtue in the main, and those who do not. For though only the heroic souls of which I have just spoken represent man at his highest, yet Conrad is willing to allow sufficient merit to some lesser spirits to admit them into his category of "good" men as distinguished from bad. Sometimes they fail consistently to maintain their ideal of virtue, from some weakness or conflict in themselves, like the heroes of *Lord Jim* or *Under Western Eyes*; sometimes they are simple loyal natures unable to take a lead in the moral battle but able to follow those who do. Most of the ship's crew of *The Nigger of the Narcissus* or *Youth* belong to this category. Conrad is charitable enough to

admit that a large number of human beings have it in
them to fight on the side of right in the moral battle,
given the right lead and allowing for an occasional failure.

Over against them, however, are ranged the armies of
the wicked. The wicked army is made up of those who
consistently and actively repudiate the moral instinct
implanted in their breast—who live without honour.
They are of two types. First of all, there are the abject:
Schomberg in *Victory*, Massey in *The End of the Tether*,
Donkin in *The Nigger*, for example. Those fail from a
weakness that expresses itself as vanity and cowardice.
They have no moral ideal; the world to them is just a
place in which feebly to pursue one's own selfish advantage, regardless of anyone else. In so far as they do desire
to cut a figure, it is in the eyes of other people and without
reference to their own conscience. They think they have
a perfect right to be rich or influential or admired, without doing anything to deserve it; and they hate the virtuous for putting them under obligations that involve
hardship and self-sacrifice. They are full of self-pity and
self-admiration, they are always asking for more; when
a crisis comes they collapse and whine and try to save their
skins. And they try to make up to themselves for their
failures by ineffective spite and weak bullying.

Further, they let themselves become the instruments of
the second category of Conrad's evil men. These are not
weak; deliberately they reject honour. Gentleman Brown
in *Lord Jim*, Mr. Jones in *Victory*, with his air of "weary
depraved distinction," Necator in *Under Western Eyes*,
the Professor in *The Secret Agent*—different in detail,
they are yet all alike in the fact that they are, as it were,
beasts of prey in the jungle of existence. Some warp in

their nature has made them congenitally destructive. Unlike the abject, they recognize the moral ideal but only to hate it. They wish to destroy loyalty, pity, magnanimity, honour. For such are damned souls, and in Hell. Their only outlet for the hideous misery which boils within them incurably, is to try and make it universal. And they have a dreadful power. Though they destroy themselves in the process, it is they who drive others better than themselves, devoted Winnie Verloc, magnanimous Heyst, to despair and death.

One other category of Conrad's characters must be mentioned here—his heroines. Conrad's is a masculine world like that of any other adventure-story writer. But it is one in which women play an important part. Here again he is different from Stevenson, different because he is a foreigner. Masculine, men-of-action English writers are boyish. They are not interested in sex. But for Conrad, a Continental virility shows itself as much in a man's capacity for passion as in his love of action. Just because they are born fighters, Conrad's heroes are also born lovers. Continental types of lover too! To most classical English novelists love is, as Fielding phrases it, a "rational passion," a tender sentiment for a virtuous object, founded largely on esteem, precious for its power to elevate life and sweeten character but always under the ultimate control of reason and virtue. Not so with Conrad. For him love is a violent force breaking in on life from no one knows where, wholly to possess a man's senses and imagination. It is an illusion—like everything else—an illusion glorious and fatal, irresistible and disruptive, leading sometimes to good, but more often to harm; one of the most formidable of all the powers which man has to encounter in the battle of existence.

In Conrad's dramas love inevitably plays a major role. As a consequence, woman, the object of man's passion, is a major character in his stories. He conceives her, however, in the light of this conception of the part she plays in human affairs. Women are part of a man's world, envisaged from a man's point of view. Not only are women objects of love, they themselves are primarily lovers. Not, it is true, always lovers in the sexual sense: Winnie in *The Secret Agent*, for example, is ruled by her maternal devotion to her idiot brother. But she, as much as the heroines of his love stories proper, is directed by her heart. Woman is born to love man—as wife, or mistress or mother or sister. And for her this love takes the place in the moral system which for Conrad's men is occupied by honour. Love bounds their horizon. They do not understand the masculine world in which they find themselves; its soldierly preoccupation with questions of duty and fidelity to some personal ideal of conduct is beyond their ken. They only know that they love one of these unaccountable creatures and are prepared to sacrifice everything in order to ensure his happiness and retain his affection. Jewel in *Lord Jim* would give her life for Lord Jim, but she cannot make out the conception of personal honour which forces him to leave her to meet his death. Only two of Conrad's heroines, Miss Haldin in *Under Western Eyes* and Antonia in *Nostromo*, guide their lives by the light of a more abstract ideal; they are both heroic patriots. Even so the quality of their sentiment is like that of his other heroines: a pure, selfless, personal devotion, unweakened by intellectual questionings, uncorrupted by egotism. They are like nuns who have repudiated the love of man to become the brides of Christ; their devotion to their country is the sublimation of the devotion that more normal women pour out on an individual male.

The themes of his stories are equally an expression of his philosophy of life. Sometimes they simply explore one aspect of it. *Youth* is a sustained paean in praise of the young man's romantic sense of glory which enables him without effort to rise victorious and high-hearted over the fears and despondencies engendered by the inevitable danger of the human situation. *Heart of Darkness* portrays the other side of the picture, and shows how the original sin in the nature of the universe, symbolized by the horror of the African jungle, destroys those characters who have no inner integrity with which to sustain themselves; *Typhoon* tells us how even a stupid man, because possessed of this inner integrity, can rise to a heroism of mythical proportions.

In his long books the drama turns on a more complex conflict in the soul of one or more figures drawn at full length. Heyst in *Victory*, Decoud in *Nostromo*, are men clear-sighted enough to see the futility of most human effort and the vanity of most human ideals and who seek therefore to live detached from the human struggle. In vain; that capacity to feel, which is the sign they are alive, inevitably forces them back into it. Unconvinced intellectually of any reason for which to fight, they are yet forced to do so by the sheer pressure of the human instinct within them.

But Conrad's most typical dramas are, as might be

expected, concerned with the question of honour. Lord Jim loses his in a moment of weakness and he spends the rest of his life seeking to find an opportunity to redeem it. Nostromo, whose sense of his own trustworthiness is inextricably bound up with the admiration which it gains him among his fellows, suddenly finds the most heroic of his acts unappreciated. This breaks the mainspring on which his virtue depended; because he is not honoured for maintaining the trust assigned to him, he betrays it. But though he keeps his betrayal secret, the knowledge of his unworthiness poisons his life and he dies despairing. For Lingard in *The Rescue* and Karain in the story of that name, the conflict is between honour and love: in a moment of weakness brought on by passion, each betrays his sworn faith. So also does Captain Whalley in *The End of the Tether*: to get enough money to assist his poverty-stricken daughter, he conceals the fact that he is going blind and is therefore no fit person to be trusted with the command of a ship. The anonymous hero of *The Secret Sharer*, on the other hand, true to his duty as a sailor, saves the ship of which he is mate, at the cost of the life of an unworthy member of his crew. His tragedy is that, for this honourable act, he is repudiated and cast out by his ignoble fellow seamen.

It will be seen that the two strains of Conrad's inspiration do not work against each other. On the contrary, the adventure-story writer in him provides just the material best needed to dramatize his particular type of philosophy. It is right that he should write of lawless regions of battle and revolution and storms at sea, where man has nothing to depend on but his own individual virtue. For to him, ultimately, all human existence is of this nature.

Heyst on his lonely island may stand for all sensitive disillusioned persons who seek to escape entanglement in the human conflict. Lord Jim fighting to retrieve his lost honour amid a crowd of alien barbarians, is in reality no differently situated from any other heroic soul seeking its salvation in this chaotic world; Mr. Curz, corrupted by the elemental evil of the African jungle, is only an extreme example of what may happen to anyone brought up stark against the ultimate evil latent in any human society. And the ships, which are the settings for so many of Conrad's most magnificent conceptions, are a superbly apt symbol of his vision of human life. What is this but a voyage through a dark uncharted ocean beset with perils; and in which man's ultimate worth is tested by the manner in which he encounters them. In a passage at the end of *The Nigger of the Narcissus* Conrad states this analogy openly. The crew have been paid off, we take a last look at them as they disperse on the dock by Tower Hill.

But at the corner I stopped to take my last look at the crew of the *Narcissus*. They were swaying irresolute and noisy on the broad flagstones before the Mint. They were bound for the Black Horse, where men, in fur caps with brutal faces and in shirt sleeves, dispense out of varnished barrels the illusions of strength, mirth, happiness; the illusion of splendour and poetry of life, to the paid-off crews of southern-going ships. From afar I saw them discoursing, with jovial eyes and clumsy gestures, while the sea of life thundered into their ears ceaseless and unheeded. And swaying about there on the white stones, surrounded by the hurry and clamour of men, they appeared to be creatures of another kind—lost, alone, for-

getful, and doomed; they were like castaways, like reckless and joyous castaways, like mad castaways making
merry in the storm and upon an insecure ledge of a treach-
erous rock. The roar of the town resembled the roar of
topping breakers, merciless and strong, with a loud voice
and cruel purpose; but overhead the clouds broke; a flood
of sunshine streamed down the walls of grimy houses.
The dark knot of seamen drifted in sunshine.

Even in the apparent safety of civilized England, Conrad suggests, the seaman is still castaway, making merry
with imminent disaster at his very feet; the roar of the
town is like the roar of those thunderous seas through
which he has been voyaging in continual peril of his life.
Conrad's world of hurricane, jungle, brigandage, and
exotic strife is a true image of the real world; for it reveals
openly what is, in fact, always and everywhere the fundamental truth of the human predicament. The adventure
tale is a most accurate parable of the human drama.

But of course the fact that it is such a parable modifies
Conrad's way of treating it profoundly. Since the adventure story was interesting to him for the spiritual significance it might contain, he presents it to us subjectively.
We see it through the eyes of the actors and also through
the eyes of Conrad watching them. This alters its character. The swift events are slowed up, the simple issues are
refined, the elemental unself-conscious figures become the
subject of subtle analysis when they are reflected in the
mind of a complex, questioning observer. With this complex vision goes a complex mood—partly tragic, wholly
ironic. Tragic because it is both grand and sad; Conrad's

prevailing sentiment has, like that of all great tragedians, the tension that comes from a simultaneous realization of the dignity of man's nature and the dreadfulness of his predicament. His irony, too, was an inevitable result of his perception of the difference between man's disposition and his circumstances—and also of the essential incongruities to be found in his innate disposition. Lord Jim's obsessed determination to redeem his honour was egotistic as well as noble: everyone else, including the girl he loved, had to be sacrificed to it; it was partly because Captain MacWhirr was so comically lacking in imagination that he was able to face the typhoon with fortitude; Winnie Verloc's beautiful capacity for self-sacrifice is devoted to preserving the life of an idiot, in reality better dead. Wherever he looks, Conrad finds matter for his irony; a very personal irony soaked in the colour of his temperament so that whether it is bitter or gentle, it remains stately and aloof, disclosing itself by no sharp deflating phrase, but by its tone of extravagant mock ceremony. "They appeared to live in a crazy maze of plans, hopes, dangers, enterprises, ahead of civilization, in the dark places of the sea; and their death was the only event of their fantastic existence that seemed to have a reasonable certitude of achievement."

II

Conrad's range of interest, then, is not private and domestic but public and cosmic. Though he believed so deeply in the individual, his interest lay in exploring the relationship of the individual to something impersonal;

to fate and nature or whatever phrase may be used to symbolize the inhuman forces conditioning man's existence on this planet; and, in a lesser degree, to life in its political and collective aspect. Even his ironic comedy is, as we have seen, a sort of cosmic comedy, arising from his sense of the incongruity of man's desire with his destiny. He had the imagination appropriate to such a range. It was powerful enough for one thing; every aspect of Conrad's world is coloured and vivified by the idiosyncrasy of his personal vision. What then are the characteristics of this vision? First and foremost, it is aesthetic in the simplest, most exclusive sense of the word. Here we come to the third element in Conrad's composition. In addition to the Stevenson and the Hardy strains in him there is a strong Henry James strain. He had an intense appreciation of the beautiful, both in life and art; and he thought that the novel should be an expression of this appreciation. It might have its value as a record of fact or comment on life. But this value is insignificant unless it is also a beautiful object in itself, like a sonnet of Shakespeare or a picture by Raphael; and the first action of his imagination, when it got to work on his material, was to transmute it into an object of beauty. This appears both in the way he conceives the stories and in the form in which he seeks to embody this conception.

Here, incidentally, was another reason why he preferred to write of picturesque events and spectacular settings. They obviously offered more opportunity for the effects of beauty; particularly the sort of beauty that appealed to Conrad. Once more his Continental origin reveals itself. His taste was unashamedly full-blooded

and romantic, delighting in the gorgeous, the exotic, the
sensuous and mysterious, in brilliant colour, sublime outlines and glittering light and grandiose gesture. Like all
romantics, beauty was to him always associated with
strangeness. It had something intensified and extravagant
about it, and generally something alien and wild as well:
the savage splendour of the Far East, the inhuman magnificence of the ocean in tempest. More often than not
he chooses such scenes as his settings: even when he writes
about modern Europe, he singles out and intensifies such
elements in his scene as have a touch of glamour and
strangeness about them. London in *The Secret Agent*
with its back streets and shady shops might seem a drab
enough subject in itself. But not as Conrad presented it.
Every light is heightened, every shadow made sharp and
dark and sinister; the whole is suffused with a fantastic
macabre beauty: so that it becomes a murky, mysterious
jungle where, amid smoke-blackened brickwork and
gleaming gaslight and driving rain, the savage Heart of
Darkness reveals itself as ominously as in the uncharted
African forest. To give his books the power to stir the
reader's imagination in the same way that a poem or a
piece of music does, Conrad screws up every key of his
instrument to the highest pitch; so that though the impression he makes may be grim it is never ugly or mean.

Nor intellectually uninteresting: so strong a feeling for
the sensuous often goes with a lack of intellectual activity.
But Conrad's intelligence is always at work, reflecting,
interpreting, drawing conclusions; so that we see the
object he describes enlivened by the quivering light shed
on it by the incessant action of his acute mind. Finally
intelligence and aesthetic sensibility are always checked

and controlled by his sense of reality. The London of *The Secret Agent* may be more dramatically illuminated than that of the London that most people see, but it is the real place.

The Assistant Commissioner, reaching this conclusion, entered the street in his turn, and came upon a large van arrested in front of the dimly lit window-panes of a carter's eating-house. The man was refreshing himself inside, and the horses, their big heads lowered to the ground, fed out of nosebags steadily. Farther on, on the opposite side of the street, another suspect patch of dim light issued from Mr. Verloc's shop front, hung with papers, heaving with vague piles of cardboard boxes and the shapes of books . . . By the side of the front window, encumbered by the shadows of nondescript things, the door, standing ajar, let escape on the pavement a narrow, clear streak of gaslight within.

Behind the Assistant Commissioner the van and horses, merging into one mass, seemed something alive—a square-backed monster blocking half the street, with sudden iron-shod stampings, fierce jingles, and heavy, blowing sighs. The harshly festive, ill-omened glare of a large and prosperous public-house faced the other end of Brett Street across a wide road. This barrier of blazing lights, opposing the shadows gathered about the humble abode of Mr. Verloc's domestic happiness, seemed to drive the obscurity of the street back upon itself, make it more sullen, brooding and sinister.

Look how Conrad's imagination modifies his subject matter. In itself the sordid little shop is not an object to stir the fancy. It becomes so first through the precision with which Conrad discriminates the aesthetic aspects of the scene; and secondly by the atmosphere of ironical fantasy with which he suffuses his picture. Disillusioned observation and romantic sensibility fuse to present the reader with a new and complex harmony.

Incidentally its author's taste in beauty enables him successfully to solve one of the outstanding technical problems which have troubled novelists during the last fifty years: namely, to reconcile two apparently divergent tendencies. On the one hand, they have wanted to be much more realistic than the classical novelists of the eighteenth and nineteenth centuries, to follow truth however far it led them from the conventional order of old-fashioned fiction. But equally they have wanted to elevate and intensify the novel so that it acquires the concentrated force and beauty of poetry. Since reality is seldom orderly and beautiful, they have found it very difficult to satisfy both these aims. Conrad, at his best, is one of the few writers who has managed it. He has been rigidly true to describe fundamental reality as he sees it, but he has always chosen to write of it in places and situations which are in themselves stirring to the aesthetic imagination. So that by simply relating the facts as eloquently as he could, he has achieved a result which is both realistic and poetic.

The Nigger of the Narcissus is an accurate account of a merchant ship's voyage without idealized characters or conventional plot of any kind. But its setting is such as to make its effect Homeric. Of course this is a specialized sort of solution, only to be attempted by someone with Conrad's peculiar experience. Not all authors can be merchant seamen. Still it does illustrate the often forgotten truth that if you want to create an effect of beauty, you will do best to choose a subject which has something beautiful in it.

Conrad's aesthetic impulse appears as much in the pattern he imposes on his subject matter as in his imaginative apprehension of it. Here it is that his kinship with Henry James is most apparent. He is no mere storyteller who begins at the beginning and goes on till the end; but a sophisticated and conscious artist with an ideal of form, to attain which he applies a subtle and elaborate craft. Each book is conceived of as a whole, centering round a single presiding theme: and every character, every incident, is designed in some way to illustrate this theme. To contrive this in the most effective fashion was of endless interest to him. He was a natural virtuoso, fascinated to experiment in form, and his works present a steady development from the relatively simple narrative of his earliest works through the elaborate constructions of his middle period, to the more controlled simplification of his last phase. A relative simplification: Conrad's vision was too complex ever to find appropriate expression in the directness of a Defoe. The point of view from which a story should be told is to him an obsessing problem, for instance, and he has every sort of device for solving it. Sometimes he tries the first person. But that affords too little chance for the full display of his irony: if the narrator is an actor in the plot he will not see it with enough detachment. On the other hand, direct impersonal narration might, he thought, break the illusion: Henry James put this idea into Conrad's head. In his middle period he is determined to avoid it; and to do so invents a narrator,

Marlowe, the spectator of the events, though not an actor in them, who relates the plot in conversation.

Again, in his wish to focus the reader's interest on the significance of the events he describes rather than the events themselves, Conrad liked to tell a story by a curious two-steps-forward, one-step-backward method. The reader is shown a character or an event; then Conrad, or the narrator who represents him, goes back and tells you the previous history which explains them. He then jumps forward to a later stage of the drama and then once more goes back for another explanation. All is designed to direct the reader's attention to the idea which is the germ of the story, and also to give him the aesthetic satisfaction that comes from the contemplation of a shapely and integrated work of art. At no moment does the author, as it were, let himself go in improvisation. All is calculated toward a conscious purpose.

These two aspects, formal and imaginative, of his creative impulse show themselves conspicuously in certain aspects of his work. The characters first of all. Conrad's range of characters is limited, as we have seen, both by his experience and by his themes. The most memorable ones fall into the categories I have mentioned. They are men of action or women of passion and they are honourable or dishonourable. The honourable are simple, faithful souls like Captain Whalley and Captain MacWhirr, or complex torn spirits like Lord Jim and Captain Anthony in *Chance*; the dishonourable are cringing abjects like Donkin and Massey or predatory, malignant demons like Jones or the Professor. In contrast to them are portraits of detached ironists vainly striving to be neutral in the human struggle, Decoud and Heyst: Conrad has clearly put much of himself into these two. But good, bad, and neutral alike, they are distinguished by the fact that they are dominated by a ruling passion which directs the course of their existences. The apathetic and devitalized have no place in Conrad's gallery. His imagination was too high-powered to find inspiration in them: and besides they do not illustrate the central action of the human drama as he conceives it. Within these limitations, however, Conrad's range of character is wide. His simple heroic sailors, Whalley, MacWhirr, Peyrol,Captain Beard, are intrinsically different from one another; sinister Gentleman Brown is a different kind of devil from sinister Mr. Jones.

Only the heroines tend to fall into a type that repeats itself. Surely, one asks oneself, the world cannot be so full, as Conrad suggests, of speechless, enigmatic, passionate young girls? Yet it may be that he intends a deliberate effect by the generalized way in which he portrays them. Their role is to be the object of the hero's love, and therefore they are always portrayed as through the eyes of the lover. Their charms, physical and personal, are conveyed with an intense vividness; we can see their sparkling dark eyes, hear the very accent of their fresh seductive voices—Conrad always lays great emphasis on the charm of the feminine voice. But the trembling glow of emotion which surrounds them at once conceals the hard outlines of their characters and transfigures them to a generalized symbol of the source and object of male passion; so that their role in that drama of masculine life, which is Conrad's subject, is kept precise and unmistakable.

With this salient exception, however, his chief characters are all individualized sharply enough. He relies on

two devices to bring this individuality home to us. First
a clear image of their appearance and voice and manner;
Conrad is a very visual writer, who is always out to make
us see his characters. His power of observation picks
unerringly on those elements in their external man which
makes them individual.

Old Singleton, the oldest able seaman in the ship, sat
apart on the deck right under the lamps, stripped to the
waist, tattooed like a cannibal chief all over his powerful
chest and enormous biceps. Between the blue and red
patterns his white skin gleamed like satin; his bare back
was propped against the heel of the bowsprit, and he held
a book at arm's length before his big, sunburnt face. With
his spectacles and a venerable white beard, he resembled
a learned savage patriarch, the incarnation of barbarian
wisdom serene in the blasphemous turmoil of the world.
He was intensely absorbed, and as he turned the pages an
expression of grave surprise would pass over his rugged
features.

This passage illustrates that mixture of realistic observation and imaginative strangeness which is the hallmark
of Conrad's genius. With eyes fixed on his subject, he
picks out the characteristic detail, the white satin skin,
the "big, sunburnt face," and then he illuminates the facts
by the light of a bold poetic image. Singleton resembled a
"learned savage patriarch." One element in the description makes it real; the other endows it with imaginative power. The Finnish sailor in the same story stands
amid his noisy shipmates of whose language he does not

understand a word "limp and dull, like a deaf man without a backbone"; the wasted head of the dying Negro
"resembled a disinterred black skull fitted with two restless globes of silver in the sockets of eyes."

With equal certainty Conrad evokes a character's
manner and voice: Heyst's courtly bow, "like that of a
prince visiting another prince on a private occasion,"
Lord Jim's "deep loud tones" that "displayed a kind of
dogged self-assertion that had nothing aggressive about
it . . . and was directed apparently as much at himself as
at anybody else."

Conrad makes his characters vivid by the skill with
which he portrays their outer man. They are given depth
and substance by the certainty and subtlety by which he
indicates their relation to the moral system of which they
form a part. Singleton has a body and a voice; he also has
a soul. We are shown the precise quality of his fidelity to
his obligations as a seaman and of the elemental wisdom
he had acquired from a long life of combat with the
unappeasable sea. Instinctively he knows that the sick
Nigger will die, for his long intimacy with the forces of
nature has mysteriously made him free of their secrets.
With greater elaboration Conrad analyzes the moral
structure which underlies and shapes Lord Jim's tormented spirit; his obsessing sense of duty, part noble, part
egotistic, his heroism which is partly romantic folly, that
strain of cowardly weakness in him which yet springs
largely from the superior sensitiveness of his imagination.
Or Decoud, the ultimately faithless man, who can think
and act positively enough when his vitality is stimulated
by the presence of others; but who, when left alone with

himself on an island, commits suicide, for he has discovered that there is no principle of belief in him to keep alive the will to live.

This method of drawing characters is, of course, especially suitable for Conrad's type of tale. On the one hand, a mere record of appearances would not be sufficient to vivify a character if we were not also shown it in violent and decisive action. On the other, violent action is necessary to give play to those heroic virtues and vices with which Conrad's moral system is concerned. For his purpose it is the perfect method. His power of observation makes his characters vivid and human—people, not symbols; his grasp of the fundamental in their moral nature makes him able to reveal them as rising convincingly to the heroic and tragic plane on which his drama moves. Lord Jim is a recognizable young Englishman we should not be surprised to encounter in the street; and yet, without losing a particle of his individuality, he can go to his death irradiated with the imaginative grandeur of a Hector or a Launcelot.

Similar characteristics mark Conrad's other conspicuous talent, his power of depicting his scene. This shows in his actual narrative. He is a first-rate storyteller, and once more he holds us by the mingled exactness and imaginative force with which he visualizes a scene, and by the unexpected images he uses to bring it before our eyes. As it wends its way down the tropical river, the boat in *Heart of Darkness* is attacked by savages.

Something big appeared in the air before the shutter, the rifle went overboard, and the helmsman stepped back swiftly, looked at me over his shoulder in an extraordinary, profound, familiar manner, and fell upon my feet. The side of his head hit the wheel twice, and the end of what appeared a long cane clattered round and knocked over a little camp-stool. It looked as though after wrenching that thing from somebody ashore he had lost his balance in the effort. The thin smoke had blown away, we were clear of the snag, and looking ahead I could see that in another hundred yards or so I would be free to sheer off, away from the bank; but my feet felt so very warm and wet that I had to look down. The man had rolled on his back and stared straight up at me, both his hands clutched that cane. It was the shaft of a spear that, either thrown or lunged through the opening, had caught him in the side just below the ribs; the blade had gone in and out of sight, after making a frightful gash. My shoes were full; a pool of blood lay very still, gleaming dark-red under the wheel; his eyes shone with an amazing lustre.

Note the accurate vividness with which every detail of the scene is drawn; you would think Conrad had been there. Yet it is not a mere photograph. It is made strange and significant by the images and epithets with which it is related; the spear "like a cane" the "extraordinary, profound, familiar glance" which the dying man casts over his shoulder as he falls.

These effects depend largely upon Conrad's phrasing. Indeed, his style is the most immediately striking of all his gifts. Conrad, out to give fiction the intensity of poetry, sought to express himself in words of a poetic concentration and felicity. He was not always successful. He does not maintain the sharp unerring sensibility to the quality of language which characterizes a writer like Virginia Woolf. His writing is sometimes clumsy, and sometimes inflated. Intoxicated by resounding polysyllables like "illimitable" and "unconquerable," he will now and again scatter them over the page without sufficient regard for their sense; so that though at first we are spellbound by the majestic din he has evoked, a second reading exposes it as a trifle hollow.

But for one failure as a stylist Conrad makes twenty superb successes. As the passages quoted show, his most powerful instrument is his use of image and epithet; image and epithet at once accurate and surprising. The commonplace is compared with the strange, the small with the great, the concrete with the abstract. Conrad speaks of "the shrieking ghost of a railway engine that fleeing in a white trail of steam seemed to vanish in a breathless, hysterically prolonged scream of war-like triumph," of hung-up suits of oilskin "swinging out and in, lively and disquieting like the reckless ghosts of decapitated seamen, dancing in a tempest," of a "yellow round face with wide nostrils, like a fierce full moon." Note the epithets here as well as the images; epithets also both unexpected and accurate: "fierce full moon," "reckless ghosts." Conrad has a typical and effective method of linking two apparently incongruous adjectives together, as when he speaks of the "blinding and frigid" light of an arc lamp, of a Negro's face "pathetic and brutal." Sometimes the unexpectedness lies in the relation of the adjective to the noun—the "impertinent mournfulness" of James Waite's stare, the "heavy seas of winter flashing in the cold sunshine." Or of the verb to the adverb; a cat "leaping sedately" over the deck, humourless little Fyne "bounding gravely" upstairs. Once again, realism and imagination fuse to convey a fresh ironic vividness.

The other characteristic element in Conrad's style is its movement. It is a speaker's style: we hear the voice rising, pausing, emphasizing, interrupting itself to exclaim or to comment: and the rhythm is modulated all the time to express the spontaneous movement of the speaker's feelings. But the speaker is an orator, not a conversationalist. The unit of rhythm is rolling, majestic, spreading out in great waves of sound as if designed to rouse tears and cries and cheers from a vast crowd. Conrad is a rhetorician. His grandiloquent taste combines with his deliberate aestheticism to make his eloquence a conscious art that, scorning to conceal itself, openly summons to its service the whole full orchestra of rhetorical effect that it may achieve the grand manner. And whatever his defects, he does achieve it. We can search the whole long line of his books in vain for a mean phrase or a lame cadence. His muse moves cumbrously but never without a slow ample grace. Nor for all her ceremoniousness is hers a frigid beauty. As the tide of emotion rises in Conrad, so do the tones in which he speaks begin to throb with a passion that irresistibly communicates itself to the reader.

I pulled back, made fast again to the jetty, and then went to sleep at last. I had faced the silence of the East, I had heard some of its language. But when I opened my eyes again the silence was as complete as though it had never been broken. I was lying in a flood of light, and the sky had never looked so far, so high, before. I opened my eyes and lay without moving.

And then I saw the men of the East—they were looking at me. The whole length of the jetty was full of people. I saw brown, bronze, yellow faces, the black eyes, the glitter, the colour of an Eastern crowd. And all these beings stared without a murmur, without a sigh, without a movement. They stared down at the boats, at the sleeping men who at night had come to them from the sea. Nothing moved. The fronds of the palms stood still against the sky. Not a branch stirred along the shore, and the brown roofs of hidden houses peeped through the green foliage, through the big leaves that hung shining and still like leaves forged of heavy metal. This was the East of the ancient navigators, so old, so mysterious, resplendent and sombre, living and unchanged, full of danger and promise. And these were the men. I sat up suddenly. A wave of movement passed through the crowd from end to end, passed along the heads, swayed the bodies, ran along the jetty like a ripple on the water, like a breath of wind on a field—and all was still again. I see it now—the wide sweep of the bay, the glittering sands, the wealth of green infinite and varied, the sea blue like the sea of a dream, the crowd of attentive faces, the blaze of vivid colour—the water reflecting it all, the curve of the shore, the jetty, the high-sterned outlandish craft floating still, and the three boats with the tired men from the West sleeping, unconscious of the land and the people and of the violence of sunshine. They slept thrown across the thwarts, curled on bottom-boards, in the careless attitudes of death. The head of the old skipper, leaning back in the stern of the long-boat, had fallen on his breast, and he looked as though he would never wake. Farther out old Mahon's face was upturned to the sky, with the long white beard spread out on his breast, as though he had been shot where he sat at the tiller; and a man, all in a heap in the bows of the boat, slept with both arms embracing the stem-head and with his cheek laid on the gunwale. The East looked at them without a sound.

I have known its fascination since; I have seen the mys-

terious shores, the still water, the lands of brown nations,
where a stealthy Nemesis lies in wait, pursues, overtakes
so many of the conquering race, who are proud of
their wisdom, of their knowledge, of their strength. But
for me all the East is contained in that vision of my youth.
It is all in that moment when I opened my young eyes on
it. I came upon it from a tussle with the sea—and I was
young—and I saw it looking at me. And this is all that is
left of it! Only a moment; a moment of strength, of
romance, of glamour—of youth! . . . A flick of sunshine
upon a strange shore, the time to remember, the time for
a sigh, and—good-bye!—Night—Good-bye. . . .

III

Conrad's style epitomizes his talent both in its strength
and in its deficiencies. For he had his deficiencies. His
imagination shows the defects of its full-bloodedness; its
texture is sumptuous rather than fine. He prefers to work
in rich colours and glossy materials. Further, though he
thrills and excites and stirs, he does not touch our hearts
with the unself-conscious, intimate authenticity of the
highest tragedy. Even those scenes of tragic heroism,
which should be his forte like the death of Lord Jim, do
not reach the level of the supreme masterpieces in their
kind, the death of Henchard, the trial scene in *Waverley*.
Somehow the characters do not achieve the independent
actuality that makes us feel we are witnessing something
not in literature but in life. For Conrad's art is not self-
effacing enough. He never lets the characters speak for
themselves. In fact his limitations are the characteristic
limitations of the conscious rhetorician that he was. Always we are aware of the man behind the work, contriv-

ing, manipulating, heightening lights and darkening shadows. Nor, though so accomplished, was his a subtle art—much less subtle than the intellect of which it is the expression. We are moved but we know how we are being moved, and we are aware that Conrad knows it too. So that our satisfaction comes partly from pleasure in watching his virtuosity; and, as such, is not of the purest kind.

He is liable also to fall into other characteristic defects of the conscious artist. Occasionally his technique over-reaches itself by elaboration. The form is too portentous and intricate to be an appropriate vehicle for the subject. Examine *Chance*, for example. All this great apparatus of indirect narrative and movement forward and back in time does in the end defeat its object. The reader becomes so concentrated in following the complicated pattern that his attention wanders away from the drama which the pattern is designed to illustrate. Moreover, some of Conrad's devices tend to destroy their verisimilitude. His attempt to get rid of direct narrative, for instance; because he will not tell us himself what Flora is feeling at the crisis of her fortunes, he has to try to persuade us that she would confide at great length in a comparative stranger and—what makes it still more improbable—while walking with him through a crowded London street.

Chance fails for another reason. All his conscious artistry did not prevent Conrad from sometimes falling into the most fatal pitfall which besets the steps of the novelist: choosing subject matter which leads him outside the true range of his creative inspiration. As we have seen, this is the adventurous and the heroic, and the masculine.

Chance centers round the processes of feeling in a young girl, cast adrift in twentieth-century England, the victim of shabby crooks and mean, suburban respectability. Till the last section of the story, when he manages to get her onto a ship, Conrad, we feel, is never on his own ground. With the consequence that, in spite of all the intelligence he has lavished on it, the story never comes to life. *The Secret Agent* too, though a tour de force and an exciting melodrama as well, is similarly unconvincing. Its London setting is brilliantly imagined; but the spies and informers and diplomats who keep the machinery of the plot working, are drawn at second-hand and overdrawn at that. Winnie, the heroine, stands out a solitary living figure, revealing, by the very authenticity of her own flesh and blood, the staginess of the figures by whom she is encircled.

Finally, Conrad sometimes fails because he does not succeed in harmonizing the varying strains of his inspiration. In *Under Western Eyes* the moralist is in conflict with the artist. The plot relates Razumov's betrayal of his friend to the police. During this section of the novel, the plot does indeed move with all the convincing force that shows it to be the product of a genuine inspiration. But Conrad is not content to end here; for his mind, stirred as it always was by a problem of personal honour, leads him to continue the tale in order to show how the betrayal worked on Razumov's conscience. His examination of this process is interesting in itself. But the action in which he dramatizes it is all too obviously a concocted affair, furnished forth with pale repetitions of stock Conrad scenes and stock Conrad characters. Even the end of *Nostromo* suffers from something of the same failure of inspiration. Nostromo has to die, but the love intrigue with the Viola sisters, which is the immediate cause of his death, is too obviously contrived to give him a dramatic and picturesque end. The Viola sisters are pieces of machinery, and we know it. Elsewhere Conrad lets his imagination clash with his sense of reality. In his later books the commonplace characters sometimes speak suddenly and unconvincingly with all the subtlety of their creator. Who can believe that the insensitive Mrs. Fyne in *Chance* would have had the perception or the wit to describe Flora's manner as "horribly merry"?

Indeed, Conrad is at his best only when the material with which he deals happens to obey every demand of his complex personality. His sense of beauty needs some richly romantic setting to have full play; the adventure-story writer in him requires an adventure-story plot; and his cast must be drawn from that world of sailors and pioneers of whom he had personal experience. When, however, all these conditions are fulfilled, the result is magnificent and in a unique fashion; books that are at once enthralling tales, objects of gorgeous beauty and—what is more unexpected—subtle and profound comments on human life. Very few novelists appeal to the intelligence as Conrad does. None, so far as I know, are also accomplished writers of picturesque thrillers.

He brings off these complex triumphs most frequently in relatively short flights. Here was another problem set him by his conception of his art. It is extremely difficult to sustain the lyrical intensity to which he aspired for more than a hundred pages or so. *Youth, Typhoon, The Secret Share, The Nigger of the Narcissus*—these are his most effortless and characteristic successes. But twice he did succeed in working on a larger scale, in *Lord Jim* and

Nostromo. Of these two, *Lord Jim* is the more moving, *Nostromo* the more extraordinary. The incident which formed its central theme—Nostromo's theft of the treasure from the silver mine with which he has been entrusted—is expanded and developed till the story becomes a study of the corrupting effect of material interests on a whole society, the South American Republic of Costa Guana, where the story takes place. The silver mine is the source of the country's wealth. To obtain full control of it, groups and individuals are ranged in continual strife, which ultimately breaks out in civil war. The stage is thronged with figures, each related in some way or other to the central situation. There are the noble patriots, the Avellanos family; there is Charles Gould, the Englishman who owns the mine and who identifies its success with his own moral success as a character. There is his selfless wife, whom he sacrifices to his obsession; there is Decoud, the mocking sophisticated man of the world drawn into the struggle against his better judgment by his love for Antonia Avellanos; there is Nostromo himself, the magnificent peasant leader of the men whose task it is to carry the silver from the mine to the door. These are only the chief among a much larger cast drawn from all types and classes, rich and poor, noble and ignoble, distinguished and insignificant. We follow the course of all their lives as they are affected by the struggle for the silver; we see how it alters their characters and destinies; and we trace the fortunes of the Republic itself, as it moves through bloodshed and brutal civil war, at last to achieve order under the up-to-date control of American big business.

The moral is typically and ironically somber; peace and

order are achieved at the cost of spiritual death. "Material interests," so glitteringly symbolized by the silver, have ended in creating a world of smooth efficiency more soulless than the bloody chaos it has replaced. In the process, the three chief male characters, Gould, Nostromo, Decoud, have all been wrecked by some weakness which has been discovered in their spiritual structure: Gould's strain of fanaticism, Nostromo's vanity, Decoud's lack of faith. Only the virtuous Antonia and Mrs. Gould have proved invulnerable to temptation; and they are left lonely and desolate. Conrad paints on an enormous canvas astir with the complex movement of life. But his command of design is so masterful that the pattern remains absolutely clear and there is not a paragraph that does not contribute to his presiding purpose. While over the whole picture, harmonizing its diversity in a Venetian richness, is spread the golden glaze of Conrad's sense of beauty.

It is a wonderful achievement: grander if not more perfect than anything in twentieth-century fiction. And truer to reality, as we have come to view it in these last tormented years. So indeed are all Conrad's books. His contemporaries lived in a safer world than ours and could conceive of the individual pursuing his private salvation freely and little affected by the pressure of mankind in the mass. This is so no longer. War and revolution have seen to that. We know the world is dangerous; and at every turn our individual fate is impinged upon by the impersonal and the collective. Conrad's history made him thirty years before his time. All the modern words apply to him. He was a refugee, an expatriate, a displaced person. To him life showed as barbarous as it does to us. Yet—here like many of us—himself he was not a barbarian. The heir to a subtle tradition of ancient and high civilization, he found himself living in a savage world.

A disagreeable predicament; especially for an artist. For the artist seeks instinctively to extract beauty from experience, to mold his vision of life into a shapely order. How can he do this when the vision is confused and bewildering and largely ugly? Not easily, if we may judge by the dissonant and spiritless productions of some contemporary authors. But Conrad managed it. Unflinchingly he turned his gaze on what appeared a perilous chaos unrelieved by hope; and then, out of his scorn and his pity, his nobility and his disillusionment, fashioned of it an image that gleams from the cosmic blackness, with which it is surrounded, like a dusky great emerald.

THE PROSE TALES
OF WALTER DE LA MARE

"Authentic tidings of invisible things."

—Wordsworth

$\mathbf{T}$HE POET-STORYTELLER is an English phenomenon. In spite of Lermontov and Victor Hugo, it remains true that abroad the same person is seldom both novelist and poet; whereas in England the lyrical spirit has so soaked itself into the very fabric of literature that some of our most famous writers have felt it equally natural to express themselves in both modes. There is Scott, there is Hardy, there is Meredith and Emily Brontë and D. H. Lawrence.

There is also de la Mare. In him the poet dominates. This is not to say his poems are better than his prose tales. But his prose tales are of an unusually "poetic" type. A great many of them deal with fantastic material, more often thought suitable subject matter for verse. And even when this is not so, even when, as in "Crewe" or "Mr. Kempe," he writes about contemporary human beings at a railway station or a London teashop, the impression he makes is unprosaic. Incident and character alike are fanciful and mysterious, the emotional tone heightened and lyrical. Every aspect of the world to which he introduces

us is steeped in "the light that never was on sea or land,
the consecration and the poet's dream."

A very individual dream too. De la Mare's world is
composed of diverse and incongruous elements. Its cast
and setting are homely; he writes mainly about children,
old maids and bachelors, old-fashioned servants, the keep-
ers of lodging houses and small shops, living in country
towns, or placid seaside resorts, or parsonages and cottages
lost in the depths of a tranquil countryside. But—here
we come to the second distinguishing feature of de la
Mare's world—there is always something odd about them.
And it is this oddness that he emphasizes. The houses are
secret and irregular, full of dark nooks and twisting stair-
cases and dusty accumulated junk: quaint ornaments,
obscure books, dim portraits with histories attached to
them. The children are queer children, with their demure
manners and solemn eyes and heads buzzing with fancies;
the bachelors and old maids are solitary, eccentric, often
a trifle crazy; the landladies and shopkeepers are "character parts," as full of grotesque idiosyncrasy as the personages of Dickens. There is a noticeable touch of Dickens
in de la Mare's imagination.

Yet his world is not like that of Dickens. Dickens', for
all its oddness, is life-size, solid, earthbound. That of de la
Mare is elfin, haunted, gossamer; and with a curious bias
toward the miniature. Its creator is fascinated by anything small, he can gaze forever at a tiny perfection. His
most sustained work, *The Memoirs of a Midget*, has for
heroine a woman two feet high; one of his most typical
stores, "At First Sight," tells of a young man who, owing
to some physical disability, cannot raise his eyes above the
level of his knee. For the rest, his scene is largely peopled

by children, birds—especially wrens and robins—butter-
flies, spiders, glowworms, dewdrops, and snowflakes.

> What lovely things [he sings]
> Thy hand hath made:
> The smooth-plumed bird
> In its emerald shade,
> The seed of the grass,
> The speck of stone
> Which the wayfaring ant
> Stirs—and hastes on!

This stanza is intensely characteristic of its author.
When de la Mare wishes to praise God for the beauty of
His creation, he chooses microscopic examples: a seed of
grass, a speck of stone. Not that his feeling for beauty is
confined to the minute. On the contrary, it shimmers
over his whole picture of the world. But it is always in
character with the rest of his genius, always an elfin
beauty: the beauty of his heroines with their pale narrow
hands, and slanting dark eyes; of his disheveled gardens,
heavy with the scent of honeysuckle; of the strange radiant birds—these are a strikingly characteristic expression of his imagination—which come now and again, no
one knows from where, to sweep with wild call across his
landscape; of his remote tangled churchyards whence the
eye moves upward from blurred mossy gravestone to
contemplate the starry night sky or dim twilight, which
provide the setting for so many of his scenes. There is
very little full sunlight in de la Mare's world.

This goes to make its atmosphere eerie. So it should be.
Elves, if taken seriously, are eerie. De la Mare takes them

very seriously. Moreover, there are much more sinister things than elves in his universe. For all its apparent homeliness, it is a place of mystery and danger. The magic he evokes is not a comfortable magic. It disquiets the spirit as the supernatural would, if we came across it in real life. Even when it is benevolent, it is convincingly genuine, and, as such, disturbing to the sense of security. When it is evil, it has the immediate inexplicable horror of nightmare. Nightmare is the right word. For a nightmare is a dream. And, after all, the most typical characteristic of these stories is their dreamlike quality. They are as enigmatic as dreams; they have also a dream's vivid, intimate intensity.

Midgets and ghostliness, homeliness and dreams—such are the surface features of de la Mare's world. They are, however, far from being its only features. If they were, his stories would not be so memorable. De la Mare is, in the truest sense of a misused, overworked word, a symbolist. The outer world he shows us is the expression of an inner world, the external drama the incarnation of an internal drama. And that internal drama is concerned with some of the profoundest and most critical issues that confront the human soul. Indeed, de la Mare is occupied with nothing less than the ultimate significance of experience. What does life mean? he asks. What is the nature of the world we see around us? Not, at any rate, he seems to reply, what it might appear to a superficial glance. He is filled with a sense of the fleetingness, the insubstantiality of what looks so solid and permanent. Has the world indeed any objective existence, he wonders; is it not merely a reflection of our own minds, altering according to the mood and character of the observer? To de la Mare, as to Blake, what appears to one man to be a thistle, to another may be a grey-headed old man. Who can say with certainty which is right? "It seemed to him," so he says of the child hero of "Visitors," " . . . almost as if the world was only in his mind, almost as if it was the panorama of a dream."

Almost—the word is important. For de la Mare does not, in fact, take a wholly subjective view of experience. Although he doubts the evidence of his senses, he has a faith. Experience may be like a dream; but the dream has a meaning. There is a streak of mysticism in de la Mare. His central conviction seems to be that behind the insubstantial ephemeral world of matter, that we perceive through our senses, lies an eternal universe of spiritual forces, of which that material world is but the temporary incarnation. He is much concerned with death: but never as a finality, always as the gateway to another mode of existence. Not that he is blind to the facts of physical dissolution. With what force does he describe Miss M.'s horror on finding the maggot-crawling carcass of the mole. "So this is what lies in wait; this is how things are!" she cries in a flash of realization. But neither to her nor to her creator does such a spectacle demonstrate the annihilation of the soul. De la Mare has had intimations of the spiritual world far too vivid for him to doubt its existence for more than a moment.

Here he recalls Emily Brontë. In fact, this aspect of his thought derives from her. *The Memoirs of a Midget* suggests, as does *Wuthering Heights*, that a human being only finds true fulfillment in union with the one other who is his or her spiritual affinity, and that if he fails to achieve this union in life, he strives for it after death. Mr. Anon comes from the grave to claim Miss M. in the same way as Cathy comes back to claim Heathcliffe. But de la Mare's interpretation of reality is more tentative than Emily Brontë's. He makes less attempt to map the spiritual universe of which he is conscious. For him it is a dark mysterious place in which he dimly perceives benevolent and malignant forces eternally at war with each other. But which is the most powerful he does not say; because, so one guesses, he does not know.

In *The Memoirs of a Midget* good prevails. Miss M. through her own errors has caused the death of her spiritual affinity, Mr. Anon. But she expiates her sin, so that at the end the spirit of Mr. Anon is able to take her to himself. In "Seaton's Aunt," on the other hand, evil is victorious. Poor, wretched little Seaton has done no harm; yet this cannot save him from destruction at the hands of those demoniac powers of which his aunt is the loathsome instrument. Of one thing de la Mare does seem certain. Man should realize the spiritual nature of the universe; he must never forget that the material world is not the only world, or he will lay his soul open to the attack of the forces of destruction who are always lying in wait for him. The hero of *The Return*, because he has been content to live a wholly superficial and material life, creates, as it were, a spiritual vacuum in himself. In consequence the soul of a wicked and miserable suicide, many years dead, takes up its habitation within him. Miss M. nearly wrecks her life because she allows her infatuation with the false and worldly Fanny to blind her to the fact that true spiritual fulfillment can only come from her union with Mr. Anon.

Seen in relation to this vision of reality, the world revealed in de la Mare's tales assumes a deeper and more serious significance than its graceful and freakish surface might lead one to expect. His ghosts and hauntings, for instance, are no mere device to awake pleasing shudders, but symbols of his belief in the soul's immortality, its capacity to influence events in this world even after death. It is from no whim either that he chooses so often to show us his story through the eyes of a child or a childish grown-up person. Living so largely in the imagination as they do, such people are less likely than are the mature and active to be cheated into thinking that the material world is the only reality. They stand, as it were, in the no man's land between the regions of matter and spirit, aware of both and thus able to see each in its true proportion. In "The Almond Tree" we see the drama of a broken marriage as it looks to a child; "Miss Duveen" presents a tragic love affair as it takes shape in the memory of a crazed old spinster. Though neither of them grasps the superficial facts of these events as accurately and fully as the normal adult would, yet, so de la Mare suggests, they are nearer to the heart of their ultimate significance.

His whimsical mixture of the homely and the magical, too, expresses his profound sense that supernatural forces are at work everywhere, even in the most unexpected quarters. Nor does the dreamlike atmosphere of these tales indicate any wish to "escape" from reality. Dreams, he says in his long poem about them, are the work of the imagination and it is only the imagination that gives significance to reality. Indeed reality, as de la Mare conceives it, is of the nature of dream, and is thus most accurately portrayed in a dreamlike mode. Dreams themselves are just as much or as little real, as anything else in life. Nor is waking experience different in kind from that known in sleep: it is just as inexplicable and insubstantial, just as subjective. "We are such stuff as dreams are made on"—Shakespeare's line is often on de la Mare's lips. No wonder: it sums up his central belief about the nature of human existence.

To convey so unusual a vision of life, de la Mare has evolved an unusual mode of expression. The style is a complex, highly orchestrated affair, rich with imagery, freaked with archaic words and poetical turns of speech, and moving in slow, winding, incantatory rhythms. And even when, as in "The Almond Tree," the style is relatively simple, the method of narration is not. Here Henry James's influence shows itself, and de la Mare's method is at least as devious as his master's. There is very little straightforward exposition or direct statement in these tales: their events are conveyed to us mainly by hint and suggestion and implication, made still more elusive by the crepuscular opalescent haze in which de la Mare veils his scene, in order to induce in the reader the spellbound mood in which he can respond rightly to this kind of story.

It must be admitted that he does not always so respond. Only a minority of de la Mare's stories are complete successes. Sometimes he tells them so subtly and tentatively as to become unintelligible. Even the simpler stories must be read very carefully if we are not to miss their full significance; for they are presented in a continuous series of delicate, minute, unemphasized touches, all of them important, but any one of which may easily escape attention. For this reason de la Mare is better at short flights. Every page of *The Memoirs of a Midget* is marked by a beauty and originality, but as a whole it does not make the impression it should, simply because it is too long for the scale of its presentation. Reading it is like looking at a large mural drawn with the myriad light miniature strokes of a mezzotint engraver.

Finally, de la Mare sometimes fails to do equal justice to the earthly and unearthly aspects of the world. This is the problem that always faces writers whose stories move on two planes of reality. How are they to make both planes of reality equally convincing? Most come to grief over the unearthly. We believe in their stories till the magic begins. Consider Mr. E. M. Forster's tales of panics and sirens, for instance. How vividly real he makes the human beings in them, the Italian peasants, and the English on their holidays abroad! But the pagan deities who intervene to upset their lives—the sirens and the great god Pan—these are no more than faded puppets from the poetry books of the nineties, and exuding a faint stale smell of that languid period. When de la Mare errs, however, it is precisely in the contrary direction to Mr. Forster. His ghosts are always and disturbingly convincing, but his material world seems too bewitched and insubstantial to deserve its name. The reader finds it hard to distinguish between the haunters and the haunted.

However, at his best, the dual nature of de la Mare's genius is the instrument of his glory; for it enables him to succeed triumphantly on both natural and supernatural planes. No one has depicted certain aspects of the English countryside as memorably as he; at the sight of some rural overgrown lane, steeped in still summer afternoon heat, or of a desolate winter churchyard at sunset, one finds oneself exclaiming involuntarily, "Why, it's like something in a story by de la Mare."

... the snow had ceased to fall: that only a few last, and as if forgotten, flakes were still floating earthwards to their rest in the pallid light of the declining sun.

With this breaking of the clouds a profounder silence had fallen upon the dome-shaped summit of the hill on which I stood. And at its point of vantage I came to a standstill awhile, surveying beneath me under the blueing vacancy of the sky, amidst the white-sheeted fields, a squat church tower, its gargoyles stooping open-mouthed—scarcely less open-mouthed than the frosted bells within. The low mounded wall that encircled the place was but just perceptible, humped with its snow. Its yews stood like gigantic umbrellas clotted with swans-down; its cypresses like torches, fringed, crested, and tufted with ash.

No sound broke the frozen hush as I entered the lych-gate; not a figure of man or beast moved across that far-stretching savanna of new-fallen snow. You could have detected the passage of a fly. Dazzling light and gem-clear coloured shadow played in hollow and ripple. I was treading a virgin wilderness, . . .

In surroundings like these—in any vast vacant quiet—the senses play uncommonly queer tricks with their possessor. The very air, cold and ethereal and soon to be darkened, seemed to be astir with sounds and shapes on the edge of complete revelation. Such are our fancies. A curious insecure felicity took possession of me. Yet on the face of it the welcome of a winter churchyard is cold enough; . . .

He can draw character too, especially child character, with a wonderfully intimate insight, and very variously; ranging as his gallery of portraits does from the charming Nicholas of "The Almond Tree," with his ardent child's first love for Miss Grey, to the dreadful, pathetic little protagonist of "The Ideal Craftsman," callously skillful in disposing of a murdered corpse: or the two heroes of "The Trumpet," Dick and Philip. Subtly in these last two de la Mare brings out the common boyish qualities which make them friends, while also indicating the difference in their outlook and manner that came from the fact that Philip was the vicar's carefully-brought-up son and Dick the neglected love child of a village woman. Yet, true to ordinary reality as they are, it is not for this we chiefly remember them. De la Mare's imagination has enabled him to penetrate beneath their flesh-and-blood surface to reveal them as spiritual entities, to give us a glimpse of their souls. Similarly he has endued his meticulously accurate snow landscape with an individual and spiritual quality, and, by so doing, made it alive and significant.

As for de la Mare's open and avowed excursions into the world of dream and ghost, the world of "Seaton's Aunt" and "All Hallows" and "Bird of Travel," it is unsurpassed in literature. He has a Coleridge-like faculty for giving a local habitation and a name to those basic nameless terrors and ecstasies and bewilderments which lurk far below the level of consciousness. It does not mat-

ter if we do not accept his interpretation of these phe-
nomena. The rationalist may admire these beautiful,
enigmatic, disquieting stories simply for the true picture
they give of the movements of the subconscious mind.
Understood as de la Mare intends us to understand them,
they reveal a penetration into the spiritual regions of
man's experience deeper than is to be found in the work
of any other English author of this century.

Nor is their force weakened by being expressed in so
delicate and decorative a symbolism. On the contrary, it
is this that gives them aesthetic value; that turns their
truth into beauty. Even at their most dreadful, de la
Mare's horrors are too drenched in the quality of his
imagination to be merely repulsive. His visions owe their
intensity of enchanted loveliness to the fact that, however
unearthly, they are as clear as the colour of a harebell.

SOME WOMEN
LETTER WRITERS

"Everybody allows that the talent of writing
agreeable letters is peculiarly female."

—*Henry Tilney to Catherine Morland*

I LIKE to fancy myself the owner of a beechen and sequestered park and in the park a charming eighteenth-century house—red-brick Queen Anne or cut-stone Adam, I do not mind which—and in the house a brown and tranquil library where I should sit by the fire in the gathering dusk of an autumn evening relaxing over a volume from the correspondence of one of the great women letter writers. The women rather than the men. For letter writing is a private art; and private life is woman's native and triumphant sphere of achievement. To say this is often thought to imply a contempt for women. In fact, the reverse is the truth. English people are such blind worshippers of masculinity that they accept a male standard of value as the absolute standard for everyone: they take for granted that the things men do best are the things best worth doing. Because man's talent is public and professional rather than private and personal, they count private and personal talents of less value. This is not so, however. Private life is half of life; and, in some respects, the more important half, for it has to do with more intimate and individual strains in human character. If you want to know a man's efficiency, you should see him at his work; if you want to know his temper, you should see him at home. Women have more chance than men of seeing their fellow beings as they really are. They take full advantage of it; their judgment of character, for the most part, is less conventional than men's, and more acute. And they excel men in the arts of private life; the social, domestic arts of dress and decoration, of love and friendship, of entertainment and intimate talk. These arts do not give them the prestige in the world that men's arts do—how can they, seeing that they are by definition private?—but they are equally productive of delight. Tête-à-tête conversation with an agreeable woman is the perfection of human intercourse.

Now letters are the nearest one can get to it in print. No wonder some of the greatest letter writers are women. And very feminine women too: it is a notable thing that the best women letter writers are not found among those exceptional women who have rebelled against the limitations of their sex to excel in men's work. We have not got any letters from Joan of Arc, but I do not imagine they would have been very entertaining. Certainly Florence Nightingale's are not, or Madame Curie's or George Eliot's. Jane Austen is a good letter writer, it is true; but Jane Austen was as feminine as a great novelist can be. And even Jane Austen is not in the first flight of English woman letter writers. For me, these are Dorothy Osborne, Mrs. Carlyle, Henrietta, Lady Bessborough, Miss Emily Eden, Harriet, Lady Granville, and Lady Sarah Lennox. Not one of them trespassed outside the sphere of activities allotted to women in their day; and what is more, none of them, to judge from their letters, ever showed the slightest inclination to do so. Dorothy Osborne even thought it

ridiculous of the Duchess of Newcastle to write poetry.
She was right so far as the Duchess of Newcastle was concerned; but I am afraid she might have said the same
thing about Emily Brontë or Dame Edith Sitwell. This,
however, is a digression. Certainly the queens of English
letter writing talk mainly about so-called feminine interests, about their relations and friends and neighbours
and love affairs and parties, with now and again a sentence or so about books or politics or religion thrown in.
Nor are their views on these subjects very unusual ones.
They are normal human beings who see experience in the
same perspective with which it presents itself to the ma-
jority of their fellows. You will search their pages in vain
for startling opinions or unusual experiences. Why, then,
are their pages enthralling? Partly, surely, because they
are so normal. We do not have to make any violent effort
of adaptation to see things from their point of view. We
can understand them and feel that they would have understood us. Their letters give us the pleasures of recogni-
tion. When Lady Granville, for instance, says "Francis
Leveson looks very large, upright and handsome; he
speaks but little," it does not matter that we do not know
who Francis Leveson is. Have we not ourselves met num-
bers of similar persons? We can visualize him perfectly.

Again, letters gain from being personal. A letter is not
the same as an essay, though many otherwise intelligent
people seem to think that it is. To open a fat envelope
and to find it filled with a dissertation on Dante or devalu-
ation is a dreadful disappointment. Letters are personal
affairs and should, therefore, be about people; about the
writer's friends or the writer himself. His general opinions are only interesting in so far as they express his
personality. These women letter writers are saved by their

very limitations from straying beyond the true bounds of their art.

Yet, for all their normality, they are not commonplace. No commonplace person can write as they do. How beautifully terse and vivid is Lady Granville's sentence about Francis Leveson; expressed at greater length and in more cumbrous language, it would not amuse us at all. Moreover, though their interests and opinions may be ordinary, they themselves are not. Each is marked by unusual qualities of charm, humour, sensibility, observation. With the result that in their pages we are shown normality through the transfiguring, irradiating medium of a brilliant temperament and an accomplished art.

The writers themselves do not deserve all the credit for this; it was partly due to their circumstances. All grew up in leisurely and civilized societies, and all, except Mrs. Carlyle, continued to spend their lives in them. Now it is in such societies that the feminine and private arts flourish most easily. Art needs an audience; the audience for the feminine arts is men. The men must have the time, tradition, and energy to cultivate a taste for these finer pleasures, and to appreciate at their full value the women who practice them. Dorothy Osborne and the rest of them did not feel any inclination to rebel against the limitations imposed on their sex, because these limitations did not, in the eyes of the world in which they lived, put them in an inferior position. Private and social life there was looked on as of supreme importance; and of that life they were the undisputed queens, whose peculiarly feminine talents were universally accepted and admired. In consequence, they had the confidence fully and naturally to express their personalities.

Moreover, they were trained in those accomplishments

which best displayed them. From childhood, they learned to be as entertaining and perceptive and well mannered as they had it in them to become. So much so, indeed, that their art became a second nature: there is nothing artificial about their agreeability. It had grown to be the mode through which they spontaneously expressed their personality. The single characteristic they all share, in fact, is a delightful, inextricable mixture of naturalness and civilization. It is the perfect blend for a letter writer. For, though a good letter must be entertaining and well written, it must also appear, at any rate, to be effortless and unself-conscious. As Dorothy Osborne herself remarks, "All letters methinks should be free and easy as one's discourse, not studied as an oration." A letter loses its charm unless it gives the illusion of unpremeditated, intimate talk. All these women letter writers achieve this illusion. Opening any of their letters is like opening a door and overhearing a private conversation.

Which conversation appeals to one the most is surely a matter of mood and taste. In a romantic mood, Dorothy Osborne is the most sympathetic companion. She was a born lover, ardent, imaginative, tender, yet possessed of a native refinement which saves her raptures from extravagance. And she had the luck to be born in an age in which it was possible, without self-consciousness, to express passion and rapture with the lyrical grace appropriate to them. A pearly glow, as from the canvasses of Vandyke, irradiates her unstudied words of love and longing. She tells her lover Temple:

Last night I was in the garden until eleven o'clock. It was the sweetest night that e'er I saw, the garden looked so well, and the jessamine smelt beyond all perfume: and

yet I was not pleased. The place had all the charms it used
to have when I was most satisfied with it; and, had you
been there, I should have liked it more than ever I did.
But that not being, it was no more to me than the next
field.

However, one does not always feel romantic, relaxing
on an autumn evening. On the contrary, one may desire
amusement; and all the better if sharpened with a little
malice. Then would be the time to beckon Lady Granville from the shelves. Listen to her, plain, clever and
caustic, describing some guests she has been forced to
entertain for a week:

The Jerseys go tomorrow. If I was handsome, and he
not frivolous, we should certainly have a little affair together . . . As it is we flag amazingly when left to ourselves. He has a mind composed of ennui and jokes, to me
the most wearying of all compositions. They both like
me as much as they can the person in the whole world who
suits them least, and I am sure we feel at moments equal
remorse at finding our affections towards each other so
cold and dead, in the midst of so many efforts and acts of
kindness. I would risk my life for them rather than spend
a week with them.

Lady Granville was a contemporary of Jane Austen,
and her pages sparkle with a crisp and kindred irony. She
cannot repress it, even when she is speaking lovingly of
the husband whom she loves. "Granville is pulling up all
his beautiful, regular features and saying, 'Now do leave
off. It is really too foolish tiring yourself.' What an angel
he is, eating buttered roll!"

But Lady Granville is not more entertaining than subtle Lady Bessborough or brilliant, cantankerous Mrs. Carlyle, or Miss Eden, another caustic sister spirit of Jane Austen, or Lady Sarah Lennox. Lady Sarah's achievement is the most extraordinary of all, because it is the hardest to analyze. The others, for all their air of informality, are conscious literary artists, choosing their words with a deliberate eye for the apt adjective and the witty phrase. Lady Sarah just sits down and pours out news, thoughts, and feelings onto the paper, and the first words that come to her mind. Luckily they were well worth pouring out. During the long course of her varied, romantic, and satisfying life, she was loved by many men. One cannot wonder at it. The personality that emerges from her letters, naïve, warm, impulsive, and wise, has a charm which we feel all the more intimately because she presents it to us with so uninhibited a spontaneity. Here she is reflecting on life, with the mature wisdom of twenty-one years old.

Now for an account of us all. I begin by myself, because I believe you won't dislike that; besides, I have been sick, is it not ridiculous? But I am in a hopefull way, my illness being caused by too much health, & great fullness of blood, which has at times by over heating myself really made me ill; but now I am very carefull & very well, only grown thin, & as Lord Holland says, very like "halfpenny ale" . . . I am grown tall too! I have less colour, & my nose is grown long, so you may guess I am not much improved; indeed few people are with growing old. But I flatter myself I have one advantage over many people, & that is, that I tell myself every day, "I am not old, but I am passed the age of a girl, it is time for me to check my vanity, & to remember that if I don't make myself agreeable, I have no right to any attention from my acquaintance."

She need not have worried; she is still exquisitely agreeable a hundred and eighty years later, speaking to me in the firelit dusk of my fancied library.

HAZLITT'S OCCASIONAL ESSAYS

"Quand on voit le style naturel, on est tout étonné et ravi; car on s'attendait de voir un auteur, et on trouve un homme."

—*Pascal*

Hazlitt is a deceptive author. No one seems to manifest his personality more aggressively. An unmistakable individual accent is audible in his shortest sentence: he takes every opportunity to air his idiosyncrasies and prejudices and preferences. Yet when we try to analyze this personality and to define its point of view, we find ourselves baffled. His center, his essence, eludes us. His very frankness emphasizes the fact that he is an enigma.

So also do the facts of his troubled life. He was the son of a middle-class Nonconformist, brought up in an atmosphere of minority opinion and encouraged from his earliest years to be in rebellion against what is established and conservative. Not that he needed much encouragement. He was born clever, versatile, restless, and difficult; combining a vivid responsiveness to life and its pleasures, with an irritable temper and a questioning, dissatisfied intellect. It was some time before he settled down as a writer; he had tried to be a professional philosopher and a painter first. Indeed, it was largely to make a living that he went in for letters. Even then his interests were too varied and too shifting for him to be able to concentrate and sustain his inspiration for the length of a whole book. The natural unit for him was the article and the essay.

His temperament was of a piece with his mind, difficult, changeable, and enthusiastic. His first unhappy marriage was followed by the painful abortive love affair which he describes in *Liber Amoris*. This was succeeded by another unsuccessful attempt at matrimony. Meanwhile, he made a great number of friends including Coleridge, Wordsworth, and Lamb, but quarreled with pretty well all of them before long. It was not easy to keep on good terms with Hazlitt. "His manner," says Coleridge, "was singularly repulsive; brow-hanging, shoe-contemplative, strange." This was Hazlitt in a bad mood. Though on occasion morose and cantankerous, he was at other times a fascinating talker who dominated the room by the fire and wit of his discourse. Indeed, what made him so hard to live with then and so difficult to understand now was that he had a divided nature. Trying to sum up Hazlitt, one is always brought up sharp by the contradictions in him.

Is he a man of feeling or a man of thought? The answer is that he is both. In a sense he is a typical romantic who yields to every wave of emotion which passes through him, and feels justified in so doing on the ground that intense feeling is a good thing in itself. Yet his mind is never submerged wholly by his feelings. At the same time that he is yielding to them he is also analyzing them from the point of view of detached reason.

Again, Hazlitt was a believer in action. He loved the vivid, vigorous turmoil of the world: he is all for London and newspapers and theaters and prize fights, he is repelled by cloisters and academics.

You will hear more good things on the outside of a stage-coach from London to Oxford than if you were to pass a twelve-month with the undergraduates, or heads of colleges, of that famous university ... The book-worm wraps himself up in his web of verbal generalities, and sees only the glimmering of shadowy things reflected from the minds of others. Nature *puts him out.* The impressions of real objects, stripped of the disguises of words and voluminous roundabout descriptions, are blows that stagger him; their variety distracts, their rapidity exhausts him; and he turns from the bustle, the noise, and glare, and whirling motion of the world about him to the quiet monotony of the dead languages.

The bustle, the noise, and glare were the breath of life to Hazlitt. Should we call him a man of action then? On the contrary, he is a born spectator—in the thick of things, but contemplative rather than active. Nor is this a mere temperamental preference. For him the contemplative life is the highest. "The contemplation of truth and beauty," he pronounces with a splendid dogmatism, "is the true object for which we are created, which calls forth the intensest desires of the soul and of which it never tires."

To contemplate in the midst of turmoil requires detachment. Hazlitt believed in detachment. One of his most memorable essays is on the advantages of living to oneself.

What I mean by living to one's-self is living in the world, as in it, not of it: it is as if no one knew there was

such a person, and you wished no one to know it: it is to
be a silent spectator of the mighty scene of things, not an
object of attention or curiosity in it; to take a thoughtful,
anxious interest in what is passing in the world, but not
to feel the slightest inclination to make or meddle with it.
It is such a life as a pure spirit might be supposed to lead,
and such an interest as it might take in the affairs of men:
calm, contemplative, passive, distant, touched with pity
for their sorrows, smiling at their follies without bitterness, sharing their affections, but not troubled by their
passions, not seeking their notice, nor once dreamt of by
them.

It cannot be said that Hazlitt practiced what he so
eloquently preached. No one was less detached, no one
had less of the pure, serene spirit that he praises. He was
always falling in love; and love to him was a storm that
threw his whole being into disorder. His opinions were
extreme; and he held them so vehemently that he could
not keep his temper with anyone whom he suspected of
taking another view. This often happened, for it was
very hard to agree with Hazlitt. Like the nature of which
they were the expression, his opinions were divided. Po-
litically, he was on the extreme left. Napoleon remained
his hero to whom he clung with perverse loyalty even
when every sensible man in England had learnt to recognize him for the tyrant he was: this was because Napoleon
was connected in his mind with the French Revolution
for which the youthful Hazlitt had felt intense enthusiasm. Yet, though Hazlitt's political opinions looked forward, his imagination looked back. Fanatic for the French
Revolution he might be, yet he passionately enjoyed the
works of its enemies, Burke and Scott, because they

showed an imaginative feeling for the romance of the past which he, Hazlitt, shared. Though he liked some modern literature, his heart was most fully given to those books whose charm was enriched by their association with bygone ages. His character was another paradoxical mixture. He was both egotistic and extrovert, acutely responsive to the world around him, yet seeing himself always as its center. In a sense he was morbidly self-conscious, warped by the sense of inferiority—social inferiority, sexual inferiority. Yet, is there not something unusually unself-conscious in the way he lets all this appear so frankly in his works? No one ever edited his personality for publication less. Hazlitt's enthusiasm and vanities and idealism and touchiness reveal themselves as frankly as do those of a child.

Indeed, though not childish, he did remain to the end of his life immature. Here we come to the figure in his carpet, the key to his mystery. For most people native disposition is modified by subsequent experience. Hazlitt differed from most people in that he was, as it were, insulated from the effect of experience by his egotism. He was so unquestioningly the center of his own universe that he judged everyone and everything by how far they fitted in with his native disposition and temperament: with the result that though experience could disturb, it could not alter him. Whatever might happen in the great world or in his private life, Hazlitt remained the same, with his youthful enthusiasms and his youthful intransigence, making his old mistakes and enjoying his old pleasures. At middle age Hazlitt was as awkward and unmanageable and full of zest as a boy of twenty.

He grew aware of this in himself and then characteristically argued from this that it must be true of all men: "You cannot change your own character," he says in one of his later essays, "and you can never be sure about other people's." This knowledge in its turn induced in him an occasional mood of bitterness, a gust of fatalistic fury with the human lot. "Nothing keeps so well," he cries, "as a decoction of spleen. We grow tired of everything but turning others into ridicule and congratulating ourselves on their defects." These dark moods were fleeting, however. Hazlitt would wake up from them to enjoy reading and the theater and a country walk as much as he had ever done: so much so that the last words of his agitated existence were, "Well, I have had a happy life."

Perhaps! But it was an incoherent life. For the consequence of this permanent youthfulness was that Hazlitt never achieved a consistent point of view. In him nature and experience did not fuse and crystallize into a defined, consistent philosophy of life. He remained like a youth; a bundle of strong heterogeneous feelings, governed by no principle, and only united by the fact they were all expressions of the same temperament. Intelligence and observation made him acute; they never made him wise. Moreover, his egotism was of a kind to thwart his artistic fulfillment. The true essayist like Lamb or Max Beerbohm is interested in his own personality only in so far as he can use it as material for works of art; he selects from it only such elements as will contribute to this objective purpose. For Hazlitt, on the other hand, the essay exists as a means to self-expression. He sits down and delivers himself of whatever happens to be occupying his thoughts at the moment. Serious or frivolous, light or learned, about poetry or politics, or morals or sport—out it all comes, unedited and unfiltered, the spectacle of life as seen through Hazlitt's eyes, as it races past lit up by his vitality and his acuteness, distorted by his prejudices, his irritability, his egotism.

His method of work was of a piece with its inspiration. Nothing could have been less premeditated:

I have not much pleasure in writing these essays, or in reading them afterwards; though I now and then meet with a phrase that I like or a thought that strikes me as a true one. But after I begin them I am only anxious to get to the end of them because I am not sure I shall do, for I seldom see my way a page or even a sentence beforehand: and when I have by a miracle escaped I trouble myself little more about them.

Not much designing here! nor any sign that the essay will be logically constructed. Hazlitt starts with a thought; lets it suggest another one and then another one until he stops. Sometimes he pulls the threads together in a final summing-up sentence; equally often he just breaks off. Not that Hazlitt is an artless writer. Consciously and skillfully he makes use of a great many literary devices: epigram, antithesis, the telling, arresting first sentence, the apt quotation to polish a point and enrich by its attendant associations the texture of his style. But these devices are not the result of long-term planning on their author's part. Rather are they like the grace notes and cadenzas which the virtuoso spontaneously improvises during the excitement of performance.

The impression made by Hazlitt's work is what one might expect from such a man and such a method. Like

the author himself, his essays are not harmonious or re-
poseful. It is as if before our mental eye a throng of
heterogeneous, brightly coloured objects endlessly stirred
and shifted. This comes partly from his failure to plan.
Sometimes he repeats himself and goes on too long; yet
when we have finished the essay we feel as if he had not
made the most of his subject. It has the air of a fragment
of some bigger work on the same theme. In consequence
he is difficult to read for long at a time. It is always hard
to read a book that does not appear to be progressing to a
definite end; and all the more if its tone is pitched up to
the febrile intensity of Hazlitt's. There is something
monotonous and overemphatic in the voice that speaks to
us from his pages. After a time we find ourselves longing
for him, if only for a moment, to soften and slow up.

Yet we never cease to admire. For Hazlitt has all the
virtues of his defects and more. The carelessness and the
vehemence are the reverse side of an extraordinary vitality
and responsiveness. Pater and the aesthetes were always
telling man to learn to respond to every kind of experience. But they practiced less well than they preached; the
experiences they enjoyed were strictly limited. Hazlitt
lived before aestheticism was invented, and it is unlikely
he would have agreed with it. But he is a model of how
to carry out its precepts successfully. He enjoyed so
many things: *Paradise Lost*, Congreve's comedies, Mrs.
Siddons' acting, eating asparagus, going to a prize fight or
a fives match, romping along in a stagecoach, daydream-
ing alone in a country garden. Moreover, he enjoys all
these things in the same way, for he throws his whole self
into each experience. To the reading of *Paradise Lost* he
brings the gusto of the asparagus lover; he appreciates the

prize fight and the country garden with the same rich imagination and discriminating sensibility. Nor, self-conscious though he may be in other respects, is he ever self-conscious about his pleasures. Never, for instance, is he the man of intellect, condescending genially to enjoy food or athletics. His gusto too is always the expression of temperament, not principle. There is no deliberate, repellent, healthy-minded breeziness about Hazlitt. On the contrary, he is introspective and moody, and proud to be so.

He is also extremely intelligent. If it be true that a man is clever in proportion to the number of mental events that take place within him during any given space of time, Hazlitt was a very clever man indeed. Every moment of his day he seems to have been observing, questioning, drawing conclusions. "There is a pleasure in madness which none but madmen know"; or "Violent antipathies are always suspicious and betray a secret affinity"; or "We are not satisfied to be right unless we can prove others to be quite wrong." At every turn Hazlitt's mind, amid the speed of its revolutions, throws off some such kindling spark of thought. He had more thoughts in an hour than most men in a month: and even when they are wrong, they are never stupid or commonplace.

They strike us the more from the way he presents them to us. Hazlitt was a wit in the old traditional sense of the term. How brilliant is his description of Cavanagh, the fives player, in terms drawn from literary criticism!

He was a fine, sensible, manly player, who did what he could, but that was more than any one else could even

affect to do. His blows were not undecided and ineffec-
tual—lumbering like Mr. Wordsworth's epic poetry, nor
wavering like Mr. Coleridge's lyric prose, nor short of the
mark like Mr. Brougham's speeches, nor wide of it like
Mr. Canning's wit, nor foul like the *Quarterly,* nor *let*
balls like the *Edinburgh Review.* Cobbet and Junius
together would have made a Cavanagh.

But, unlike many wits, Hazlitt can also be poetical.

Horas non numero nisi serenas—is the motto of a sun-
dial near Venice. There is a softness and a harmony in the
words and in the thought unparalleled. . . . Some monk
of the dark ages must have invented and bequeathed it to
us, who, loitering in trim gardens and watching the silent
march of time, as his fruits ripened in the sun or his
flowers scented the balmy air, felt a mild languor pervade
his senses, and having little to do or to care for, determined
(in imitation of his sun-dial) to efface that little from his
thoughts or draw a veil over it, making of his life one long
dream of quiet! *"Horas non numero nisi serenas"*—he
might repeat, when the heavens were overcast and the
gathering storm scattered the falling leaves, and turn to
his books and wrap himself in his golden studies!

These passages characteristically illustrate Hazlitt's
prose. Improvised and vital, it is talker's prose, composed
of direct uninverted sentences and in a diction that does
not admit far-fetched or archaic words. But it is no
ordinary talker's prose. For though its basic texture is
plain, it is thickly embroidered all over with the flourishes
of what may be called conversational ornament: epigram,
paradox, simile and metaphor, apt quotation. Hazlitt

incessantly sharpens the point he is making by a vivid phrase or turn of wit: and now and again he indulges in a flight of talker's eloquence. Quickening under the stress of excitement, his style soars upward in a great coruscating firework flight of words expressing enthusiasm or indignation or a sort of ardent, dreamy meditation—this will sometimes involve him in a sentence a page long—and then back with a shrug and smile to earth again. Here is the end of his great panoramic description of Coleridge's intellectual pilgrimage:

But all the former while, he had nerved his heart and filled his eyes with tears, as he hailed the rising orb of liberty, since quenched in darkness and in blood, and had kindled his affections at the blaze of the French Revolution, and sang for joy, when the towers of the Bastille and the proud places of the insolent and the oppressor fell, and would have floated his bark, freighted with fondest fancies, across the Atlantic wave with Southey and others to seek for peace and freedom—
          "In Philarmonia's undivided dale!"
      Alas! "Frailty, thy name is Genius!"—What is become of all this mighty heap of hope, of thought, of learning and humanity? It has ended in swallowing doses of oblivion and in writing paragraphs in the *Courier*.—Such and so little is the mind of man.

In what other English style do we hear more vividly the actual modulations of the spoken voice and all the various moods that throb through them!
      All the same, Hazlitt's style is no more faultless than anything else about him. With the virtues of a talker's style it possesses its besetting sins. The carelessness of talk,

for one thing; Hazlitt's grammar is sometimes incorrect and his quotations often inaccurate. Moreover, he appears sometimes not to have reread his sentences aloud to test their euphony. Even in the passage on Coleridge I have just quoted there is a disagreeable jingle left: "What a *heap* of *hope*"! Sometimes, too, in the heat of his excitement, he falls into a singsong semiverse rhythm. Finally, the fact that his writing is so much like talk means that it is liable to be insufficiently paragraphed. An orderly train of thought composes itself naturally into paragraphs, each grouped round a successive point and leading with seeming inevitability from one to the other. This organization into paragraphs makes a discourse easy to read. But it only comes as the result of reflection which qualifies and imposes order on the confusion of spontaneous thought. People do not talk in paragraphs, they say first one thing and then another just as it comes into their heads. Hazlitt often writes like this; his style is composed in sentences, not in paragraphs. The result is that it is tiring to read. At its worst it tends to fall into that monotony of continual emphasis which marks the discourse of the brilliant, uninterrupted talker.

Yet, once again, virtue outweighs defect. Tiring it may be, but it is unfailingly exhilarating to listen to anyone talking with Hazlitt's especial unique blend of the happy and the effortless. Casually but with certainty he hits on the memorable right word; Spinoza searching "for the soul of all things, in some shadowy sense forlorn of meaning"; "the tall rock that lifts its head in the erectness of Wordsworth's spirit"; "Byron made man in his own image and woman after his own heart." Here are phrases to make most careful stylists sour with envy; but how

spontaneously Hazlitt throws them off! We could put
up with more imperfections in return for so delightful an
ease, so careless a confidence.

It is the ease and confidence of his own spirit. Hazlitt
is a teacher even though he never intended to be. For to
read him is to learn to take emotion naturally. This is a
lesson writers gave up teaching after his day. Since the
middle of the nineteenth century, they seem to have lost
their emotional nerve. They often feel strongly; whose
feelings could be stronger than Ruskin's or D. H. Lawrence's? But they always seem to need to defend them
on moral grounds: for them a feeling is never its own
justification. For Shakespeare and his contemporaries it
was. They were glad or gloomy according as their temper
happened to incline them. So also was Hazlitt. He can
be grave or frivolous or angry or sad all in the space of one
essay. Nor does he bother as to whether his mood is a correct one for a man of his convictions. Listen to him, the
bitter arch-Radical, talking about the peerage:

Could I have had my will I should have been born a
lord: but one would not be a booby lord neither. I am
haunted by an odd fancy of driving down the Great
North Road in a chaise and four, about fifty years ago,
and coming to the inn at Ferry-Bridge, with outriders,
white favours and a coronet on the panels; and then, too,
I chose my companion in the coach. Really there is a
witchcraft in all this that makes it necessary to turn away
from it, lest, in the conflict between imagination and im-
possibility, I should grow feverish and lightheaded! But,
on the other hand, if one was a born lord, should one have
the same idea (that everyone else has) of a *peeress in her
own right?* Is not distance, giddy elevation, mysterious

awe, an impassible gulf, necessary to form this idea in the mind, that fine ligament of "ethereal braid, sky-woven," that lets down heaven upon earth, fair as enchantment, soft as Berenice's hair, bright and garlanded like Ariadne's crown; and is it not better to have had this idea all through life—to have caught but glimpses of it, to have known it but in a dream—than to have been born a lord ten times over, with twenty pampered menials at one's beck, and twenty descents to boast of?

Imagine any of our latter-day progressives writing such a passage! George Orwell for instance: apart from the fact that he had not the high spirits, he would have been too nervous that some ill-disposed reader might think him irresponsible or snobbish; and secretly he might fear lest such a suspicion was justified. He would not have the confidence of his moods. Hazlitt always had the confidence of his moods.

Surely he was right. He perceived the nature of existence more truly than our anxious contemporaries. Life is incurably heterogeneous and incongruous, and a sensible man does not repine at this. On the contrary, he recognizes it and accepts it; and, when he can, welcomes it as an opportunity to enjoy himself more variously.

WALTER PATER

"This is that Lady Beauty, in whose praise
   Thy voice and hand shake still,—long known to thee
   By flying hair and fluttering hem,—the beat
   Following her daily of thy heart and feet,
How passionately and irretrievably,
  In what fond flight, how many ways and days!"

               —*Dante Gabriel Rossetti*

WALTER PATER, it is important to remember, was throughout his mature life a don at Oxford. Not, indeed, a typical don; he was too odd a mixture for that. This showed itself in the figure which he presented to the world. Imagine a stocky, rocky, unromantic-looking man, with a bristling moustache and dressed carefully in the sober dark broadcloth which the Victorian age thought the correct wear for members of respectable professions. But imagine also round his neck—and offering surely an infelicitous contrast to the broadcloth—he is wearing a tie of brilliant apple-green silk. Further, when he speaks, there issues surprisingly from the be-bristled lips, sentences of jeweled elaboration uttered in accents of solemn and delicate preciosity.

Now each of these things, broadcloth and green tie, moustache and preciosity, were deeply characteristic of him. He was that rare hybrid, the scholar-artist. We can easily see why it is rare. The scholarly spirit is intellectual and impersonal, and refers its judgments to standards of reason and fact; the artistic is sensuous and personal, and refers its judgments to standards of feeling and imagination. It is unlikely that the two strains should appear in the same man. If they do, he generally takes care to keep them apart. Lewis Carroll's mathematical works are very different from *Alice in Wonderland*; A. E. Housman, the professor of Latin, is not at all the same person as A. E. Housman, the Shropshire lad. But Pater the lecturer on Plato is recognizably the same man as Pater the creator of *Marius the Epicurean*. In him the two strains are twined together. He did not take off the green tie of the artist when he put on the broadcloth of the don. As a matter of fact, the tie was the more characteristic garment of the two. Pater valued things primarily for their appeal to his sense of beauty. All his most precious and memorable experiences were aesthetic experiences. They were also his most fruitful experiences. For he was not merely content to enjoy beauty, he wanted to create it. As much as a poet or a painter, he was inspired to write by the desire to incarnate a personal vision of experience in an appropriate and beautiful form.

The subject matter of his work, however, was different from the poet's or the painter's. Here it is that his academic side showed itself; it is here that we find ourselves brushing up against the broadcloth. Pater had an active, inquisitive, searching mind that instinctively sought to order and analyze impressions, and also to draw general conclusions from them. This instinct was as fundamental to his nature as was his responsiveness to beauty; so fundamental as to form an integral part of his creative impulse. The vision of beauty he wished to express was largely an intellectual vision, an intellectual vision of aesthetic experience. He was a creative critic and his subject was art.

But not art alone! In addition to being aesthetic and

intellectual, Pater was a moralist, deeply concerned to know how a man ought to live. In this, too, he was characteristic of the earnest, strenuous, puritanical Victorian age in which he lived. Pater did not, indeed, feel completely at home in it; aesthetes are not at home among Puritans. But if not puritanical, he was earnest. He did feel he ought to do something to try to justify his point of view to his conscientious contemporaries. And indeed his mind was too active to be content merely to relax and enjoy his impressions. He could not help asking himself what light his views on art threw on his views on life, and how these in turn affected his views on conduct. He was a critic not only of art but of living.

His views on both reflect his mixed nature. His aesthetic criticism was appreciative criticism. In his view certain books and pictures were subjects for criticism because they gave pleasure. The critic's task is to illuminate his pleasure by defining it and analyzing it into its component parts. He can then, if he pleases, go on to discuss the nature and views of the man and period which produced the work, or to argue from the example of art he is studying as to the nature of art in general. But he must never let these activities distract him from his primary purpose; he must always remember that historical or psychological interpretation, and general speculations too, are valueless unless they help us to appreciate particular works. Abstract discussions about the nature of beauty struck him as particularly futile; for we are only aware of beauty as embodied in particular examples. Pater also was suspicious of aesthetic dogmatism, because he had noticed that it so often meant laying down laws that excluded works of art which did in fact give a great deal of pleasure. Like Keats he aspired to love "the principle of beauty in all things." This principle, he noted, has manifested itself very diversely in various ages and various forms. The wise critic, therefore, should try to tune his taste to respond to them all.*

Pater approached life in the same spirit as he approached art. His theory of living is based on his sense of the paramount value of aesthetic experience. The most precious and memorable moments in his life had been those when he had been stirred to a sense of the beautiful. How was this to be explained? What did these moments portend? Pater's answer to these queries was not the same throughout his life. In his youth he said flatly and firmly that they could not be answered, that beauty was just something felt, and that a sensible man was content to enjoy the feeling without asking any further questions. Here again he shows the influence of the age he lived in. Till the middle of the last century, the philosophies by which most men lived were based on a belief in some absolute ideal, religious or otherwise; and lovers of beauty had justified their love by these ideals. Beauty was the revelation of the Divine Mind in all things, they said: "Beauty was truth, truth beauty." But by the time Pater grew up rationalism and scientific discovery between them seemed to many people—Pater was one of them—to have undermined the foundations of religious faith; and with it all other ideal interpretations of the nature of existence. So far from the world being a manifestation of the Divine Mind, it was an expression of some

---

*Pater's general critical theory is stated in the Preface to *The Renaissance*; but certain aspects of it are further developed in his other works, notably in the "Essay on Style" from *Appreciations*.

automatic and mechanical material force arising from no
one knew where and moving toward no one knew what.
The idea of a spiritual world lying behind the material
world was a figment of man's fancy. If this was true, it
was not possible to justify the love of beauty on ideal and
religious grounds. But, said Pater, why try? Life is just
a stream of impressions dissolving one into the other
as they float continuously through our minds. Some,
however, seem fraught with an unusual beauty and significance; while they are with us, we feel our spirits
expanded, enriched, delighted. Let our aim therefore be
to arrange our lives so that we have as many of these
precious impressions as possible. If we succeed in doing
this we have done all we can.

He proclaims in his impassioned peroration in the Epilogue to *The Renaissance*:

Every moment some form grows perfect in hand or
face; some tone on the hills or the sea is choicer than the
rest; some mood of passion or insight or intellectual excitement is irresistibly real and attractive to us,—for that
moment only. Not the fruit of experience, but experience itself, is the end. A counted number of pulses only
is given to us of a variegated, dramatic life. How may we
see in them all that is to be seen in them by the finest
senses? How shall we pass most swiftly from point to
point, and be present always at the focus where the greatest number of vital forces unite in their purest energy?

To burn always with this hard, gemlike flame, to maintain this ecstasy, is success in life.

The ideal recommended in this passage, you will note,
is contemplative and solitary. It is what a man feels and

not what he does that matters, and the feelings that matter most are not those which he shares with others but which he entertains alone in meditation. Moreover, though Pater is interested in the relation of art to morals and right conduct, his approach is very different from that of most thinkers who have considered the subject. These nearly always start with a moral system, as it were, and then judge art by how far it conforms to it. Pater starts with an aesthetic taste, and goes on to judge moral precepts by how far they satisfy that taste. He approves of goodness because it is beautiful, not of beauty because it is good. He estimates acts and opinions in the same way as he estimates works of art. This means that his standards are relative standards. A work of art is valuable if it produces an effect of beauty; and effects of equal beauty have been produced by writers with different and even opposed philosophies of living. This, thought Pater, showed that the same standards need not be right for everybody. It might be right for Plato to be intolerant and for Montaigne to be tolerant, for Watteau to be pleasure-loving and Pascal a Puritan. The worth of a view resided in the beauty it could inspire, not in its conformity to some absolute conception of truth.

So spake the young Pater. The older Pater was less uncompromising. Inevitably: Pater's gospel as expressed in *The Renaissance* rested on an unresolved discord. It said, on the one hand, that nothing in life had an absolute significance, and, on the other, that beauty gave him a sense of intense significance. Both of these propositions cannot be true. The meaningless cannot legitimately communicate a sense of meaning. The truth was that the supreme value which Pater sets on aesthetic experience is

not consistent with a purely humanistic and untranscen-
dental view of the nature of existence. Beauty, to have
the significance he attaches to it, must surely be an incarnation of something absolute and eternal: it must be, in
some sense, a revelation of divinity; in the words of Sir
Thomas Browne: "A sensible fit of that harmony which
intellectually sounds in the ears of God." Whether he
realizes it or not, the aesthete is a worshiper.

There are hints in his later work that Pater had begun
to suspect this. At the end of *Marius* he says that the
reason the soul finds the nature of existence so mysterious
may possibly be that she is a native of some other world
to which she may return, after death, to find an answer
to the riddle. He also found himself deeply moved by
religious art and religious ritual; partly because they were
beautiful in themselves, but still more, he says, because
they ennobled the plain facts of the human situation by
investing them with an ideal significance. In his study
"The Child in the House" from *Miscellaneous Studies,* we
find that religion was in his words

a sacred ideal, a transcendent vision or representation,
under intenser and more expansive light and shade, of
human life and its familiar or exceptional incidents—
birth, death, youth, age, tears, joy, rest, sleep, waking—a
mirror towards which men might turn away their eyes
from vanity and dullness, and see themselves therein as
angels with their daily meat and drink, even, become a
kind of sacred transaction.

Religion with Pater meant the Christian religion. As
time went on he also showed signs that his views were

moving slightly in a specifically Christian direction. Casually and unexpectedly at the end of the "Essay on Style," he lets fall the remark that great art differs from good art, among other things, by its power to increase our faculty for sympathy, or to reveal the glory of God. The tone in which he speaks is vague and hesitant; but the thought implies a standard of judgment noticeably inconsistent with the skeptical aestheticism of *The Renaissance*. The hard, gemlike flame has begun to veer and flicker in a Christian wind. Again, two of Pater's most intimately studied heroes, Marius and Sebastian van Storck, break off careers, up till then given up to sedulous self-cultivation, to perform sudden impulsive acts of self-sacrifice; and Pater seems to approve of them for this. How can he then still believe that the aim of life is "to be present at the focus where the greatest number of vital forces are present in their purest energy"? Self-sacrifice is a Christian virtue; and in fact Marius is represented as half-converted to Christianity on his deathbed.

Half-converted because that was the most his creator could ever manage to be: Pater never became intellectually convinced that Christianity was true. For one thing he was so imbued with the idea that truth was relative, that it was almost impossible for him to accept a creed that claimed its truth was absolute. Moreover, he had been deeply, if reluctantly, impressed by the Rationalists. This was not just because he thought their arguments strong. Pater was enough of a Victorian to believe in progress, little as he might like its visible effects. The fact that many more of his contemporaries were skeptics than were their forefathers struck him—odd as it may seem to us—as in itself a reason to think the skeptical

view was the true one. He even went so far as to say (in
his study of "The Poetry of Michelangelo" in *The Renaissance*) that Michelangelo had a deeper insight than
Dante into the nature of existence because he was more
doubtful about it. Pater was all the weaker to resist
rationalist attack because he was not fortified against it
by personal religious experience. Though he appreciated
the mystical spirit when expressed beautifully in works
of art, he was himself unmystical. His temperament was
too sensuous easily to conceive a spiritual reality that
could not be apprehended by the senses. When he says in
his essay in *The Renaissance* that Leonardo da Vinci must
have found it hard to imagine the next world because he
desired beauty "always in such precise and definite forms
as hands and flowers and hair," he is surely speaking of
himself. No—the nearest he got to Christianity was a
belief that it *might* be true. It would be very agreeable
if it was, and no one could prove it was not. For the rest,
he regularly attended church, toyed with the idea of
becoming a Roman Catholic, and wistfully wished that,
like Sir Thomas Browne or Charles Lamb, he had been
born in some earlier age, when men accepted the faith of
their fathers and forefathers without worrying.*

This was an unsettled, unsatisfactory conclusion to
come to. However, I doubt if it troubled Pater deeply.
Religious uncertainty did not touch the faith he lived by,
his instinctive, unquestioning conviction of the supreme

---

*Pater nowhere states his view on religion explicitly. It is to be
picked up from sentences and paragraphs scattered over his work,
notably *Marius the Epicurean,* "The Child in the House," the essays
on Pascal, Sir Thomas Browne and Lamb, and the review of *Robert
Elsmere* reprinted in *Essays from the Guardian.*

value of the beautiful. Nor did it weaken his impulse to express this faith in the form of a work of art. He was much concerned with the question of form, and those forms he employed were his own, freshly devised to suit his dual purpose, aesthetic and intellectual. They must give him opportunity to state his views precisely, but also in a manner that would stir the reader's imagination and delight his aesthetic sense. Pater made use of two modes for this purpose: *The Renaissance* and *Appreciations, Greek Studies* and *Plato and Platonism* are critical essays; *Marius the Epicurean, Gaston de Latour* and *Imaginary Portraits* are fictitious biographies or biographical sketches. In the critical essay the basic pattern is intellectual; Pater expounds his views and the reasons for them openly and directly. But he transfigures his statement of them by expressing them in a style deliberately designed to stir emotion and imagination as poetry does; heightened, melodious, thickly embroidered with imagery. In his fictitious biographies, on the other hand, the basic pattern is aesthetic. Picturesquely he tells the story of a personage, real like Watteau, or imaginary like Sebastian van Storck; human like Marius or half-supernatural like Denys L'Auxerrois. But—and here Pater's intellectual bias shows itself—the story is concerned less with his hero's character, and with the drama of his life, than with the ideas he holds or stands for. Some of his heroes like Sebastian and Duke Carl embody a phase of culture, others like Marius and Gaston are searchers after truth, who try one philosophy of living after another in pursuit of their quest.

The dual strain in Pater equipped him to make a success

of such books. *The Renaissance,* in particular, is the outstanding example in English of a book about works of art
which is also itself a work of art. It is admirably designed.
In the Prefatory Note Pater sets out his principles of
criticism in general, and of their application to the Renaissance in particular. He then proceeds to illustrate these
in a series of studies of artists and personalities, each of
which starts with a passage of generalization and then
modulates into an eloquent re-creation of his subject's
personality and the sentiment it stirs in him. Finally, in
the Epilogue, he broadens the scope of his vision and displays all that has gone before in relation to the fundamental problem of how to live as it presented itself to him.
The book is thus at once the expression of Pater's critical
judgment, of his moral personality, and of his aesthetic
impulse. Yet it is not heterogeneous or disparate. It has
unity, the intellectual unity of an orderly logical structure, and the aesthetic unity that comes from the fact
that every sentence of it is steeped in the colour of Pater's
imaginative temperament.

The two sides combine with equal profit when he comes
to make particular critical judgments. Unlike most
critics, he is equally distinguished by his sense and his
sensibility. This sensibility was subtle, passionate, and
various. He loved the principle of beauty in all things,
in practice as well as in theory: and he can discern it in
the most diverse manifestations. Equally he delights in
Greek and Gothic, Dutch painting and Italian painting,
the homely and the exotic, the grave and the frivolous,
Flaubert and Scott, the statues of Michelangelo and the
operettas of Gilbert and Sullivan. With an exquisite dis-

crimination he savours the particular flavour of each. But he does more than savour. His intellect is always at work to analyze each flavour into its component ingredients. Deftly he isolates that sense of wild terror and darkness that shadows and makes poignant the flights of Charles Lamb's playful, homely fancy. Subtly he discerns that mysterious, preternatural streak in Wordsworth's imagination, that sense of "unknown modes of being," whose unearthly light transfigures his pictures of simple peasant life and makes them sublime and disturbing. As he says in his essay on Wordsworth in *Appreciations*:

A sort of biblical depth and solemnity hangs over this strange, new, passionate, pastoral world, of which Wordsworth first raised the image . . . the sudden passage from lowly thoughts and places to the majestic forms of philosophical imagination, the play of these forms over a world so different, enlarging so strangely the bounds of its humble churchyards, and breaking such a wild light on the graves of christened children.

These are complex impressions: and Pater, complex himself, has an eye for the complex in others. "It is pleasant," he remarks, in *Greek Studies*, "when, looking at mediaeval sculpture, we are reminded of that of Greece; pleasant likewise in the study of Greek work to be put on thoughts of the Middle Age." Equally pleasant to his imagination is the blend of garden freshness and courtly artifice in the poetry of the Pleiade, of barbaric horror and pastoral beauty in the Bacchanals of Euripides, the fantasy of classic Apollo born anew in mediaeval France, the sense of foreboding and melancholy that casts a shadow over the elegant frivolity of Watteau's pictures. He writes of them in "A Prince of Court Painters" in *Imaginary Portraits*:

As I gaze upon those windless afternoons I find myself always saying to myself involuntarily, "The evening will be a wet one." The storm is always brooding through the massy splendour of the trees, above those sun-dried glades or lawns, where delicate children may be trusted thinly clad; and the secular trees themselves will hardly outlast another generation.

Pater does not confine his intellectual activity to analyzing the individual work. Since he sees it always as the expression of a period and phase of culture, he goes on to relate it to these. He is the most expert of time travelers, equally able to take himself back in imagination to Plato's Sparta and Montaigne's France and Spinoza's Holland, and as sharp to discriminate and analyze the quality of a period as he is of an individual. Finally, he allowed himself now and again to speculate from his experience of particular works of art as to the laws governing art in general. He does this tentatively, for, as we have seen, he deeply distrusted aesthetic lawgiving. But when he does touch on it he goes straight to the point, as in his "Essay on Style." How true is the distinction he draws between truth to fact which is the quality of good writing, and truth to the author's "sense of fact" which is the quality of fine writing! How clearly and justly he defines in art the relation of form to matter!

In his study, "The School of Giorgione" from *The Renaissance*, he says:

All art constantly aspires towards the condition of music. For while in all other kinds of art it is possible to distinguish the matter from the form, and the understanding can always make this distinction, yet it is the constant effort of art to obliterate it. That the mere matter of a poem, for instance, its subject, namely, its given incidents or situation—that the mere matter of a picture, the actual circumstances of an event, the actual topography of a landscape—should be nothing without the form, the spirit, of the handling, should become an end in itself, should penetrate every part of the matter: this is what all art constantly strives after, and achieves in different degrees.

It is the paradoxical triumph of his intellect that it teaches him never to take art too intellectually. He was clear-minded enough to see that because poetry is first of all an art like music, it has therefore more in common with music than with ethics or philosophy. He can appreciate both Flaubert and Scott because he had the wits to see that the important thing about both was not their ideas, in which they differed, but their common gift of expressing their inspiration in an artistic form. No English critic is at once so sensitive and so hard-headed as Pater; so catholic and so acute. It was the two strains in him that made him so. His artist's sensibility made him responsive; his academic intellect made him understand his responses.

But one cannot get anything for nothing in this hard world. And when Pater stops confining himself to appre-

ciation and sets up as a creator in his own right, the two
strains combine less easily. For creative writing involves,
in a way that critical writing does not, the expression of
the artist's whole personality with all its attendant idiosyncrasies and limitations: and Pater's personality and his
purpose do not always harmonize. Like his mind, his
personality was an odd mixture. Here again broadcloth
and green tie meet in curious juxtaposition. Imaginatively
he was a child of his age; a native of the nineties, a typical
contemporary of Rossetti and Burne-Jones, delighting in
the subtle, the voluptuous, the refined, the exotic; an
amateur of rare and curious flavours, enamoured, like his
own Mona Lisa, of "strange thoughts and fantastic rev-
eries and exquisite passions" ("Leonardo da Vinci" in *The
Renaissance*). But he enjoyed these things only in imagination. His temperament, as it showed itself in life, was
very different. He was a decorous, low-spirited don,
celibate and solitary, fastidiously shrinking alike from
intimacy and from adventure, detesting conflict and controversy, clinging affectionately to established forms and
traditions, and ill at ease, for long, anywhere but in England. "Between you and me and the post," he once said,
"I hate a foreigner."

These two strains combined in just the kind of complex
blend that appealed to Pater himself. Indeed there is a
charm in the thought of his figure, neat in gloves and top
hat, stepping demurely along from his college rooms to
attend a tea party in some mock-Gothic villa in North
Oxford, while all the while his head is swimming in a haze
of many-coloured, outlandish visions of maenads and
monasteries, and ethereal Fra Angelico angels, and pow-
dered Rococo princelings, and sumptuous sinful Borgias.

But it is the slightly comical charm that is born of incongruity. The two strains in Pater's personality were comically incongruous, both with each other and with his opinions. It is absurd to rhapsodize about Leonardo da Vinci to the extent that Pater does, when in life one would have avoided him as just another dreadful foreigner: there is something ludicrous in the contrast between the life of passionate experience which Pater advises us to embrace and the tone of refined languor in which he proffers his advice. The low-spirited hedonist cannot fail to be something of a figure of fun.

Did Pater realize this? I doubt it. For, though his friends tell us he was humorous, there is precious little sign of it in his writings. Here is another element in his composition which did not harmonize with his theory of the good life. We need the help of the comic spirit, if we are to view life in the same way as we view art. Life is so full of inconsistency and discord and anticlimax that, more often than not, the only sort of aesthetic satisfaction it can provide is that given by comedy or farce. Pater could not take it like this. In *Greek Studies* he speaks with approval of the "delicate laughter" that Euripides stirred in his audience; but on paper at any rate he himself never indulges in laughter, delicate or otherwise. As a matter of fact, "delicate laughter" is not the kind of phrase that is used by a man with much humour. It is precious; and preciousness goes ill with jokes. Pater's lack of humour did make him thus liable to some of the more laughable extravagancies of the aesthetic movement. There are moments when his taste for the exquisite gets out of control of his good sense, and he becomes all too like Bunthorne. Emerald and Florian are pretty names; but I cannot think them probable or appropriate Christian names for a couple of Victorian English schoolboys (in "The Child in the House" and "Emerald Uthwart"). Nor can I believe that such a schoolboy would be consoled for the death of a playfellow by the thought that this playfellow's flesh would turn into violets in the following spring. This, incidentally, is not the only time that Pater strikes a false note in speaking of the physical circumstances of death—or physical horror of any kind for that matter. He is very much aware of physical horror: his acute sensitiveness to the beautiful went along with an equally acute sensitiveness to the ugly. Indeed this was so acute as now and again to rouse a morbid excitement in him: with the result that instead of turning away from horror, he lingered over it, perversely fascinated. It is as if consciousness that the violets were growing out of a corpse added spice to his pleasure in their prettiness. Pater's taste for curious flavours sometimes led him to dwell on curiously unpleasant ones.

These quirks and limitations in Pater's personality could not be kept out of his work. No praise is too high for his critical essays so long as they stick to criticism, to defining the quality of an artist's achievement and to drawing general conclusions from this definition. He does this admirably in his English studies—on Lamb, Wordsworth, and Coleridge—for since these were his own countrymen and lived not long before he did, he finds no difficulty in entering imaginatively into them. But when, as in *The Renaissance* and *Greek Studies*, he goes further afield in space and time, the results are less convincing. For they are tinged all too strongly with the colour of Pater's creative personality. He means to identify himself with his subjects; but more often he identifies his subject with himself. Botticelli, Leonardo, Michelangelo, present themselves before us, unexpectedly and improbably, as shrinking, shy, highly cultured souls, oscillating languidly between faith and belief and with marked Oxford accents. Even when they are not like Pater himself, his personages do seem in some sort to belong to his period. The Pre-Raphaelites of Florence in 1460 appeared miraculously changed into the Pre-Raphaelites of London in 1870; in Pater's *Greek Studies*, Dionysus, Demeter, and the other classic deities emerge for all the world like figures in a picture by Burne-Jones, with nerveless limbs and fragile, pensive faces. Of course there is a gain as well as a loss in all this. Pater's individual interpretations are animated by his individual charm. To see Olympus and fifteenth-century Florence through the eyes of a Victorian Oxonian and irradiated by the ideal light of his romantic enthusiasm for them, is to see something odd and new and delightful. But it is not the same thing as seeing them as they really were.

These limitations show up even more flagrantly in his imaginative biographies. For these are stories; and to make stories convincing needs dramatic power. The author must be able to exhibit his characters in speech and action. Pater, stiff, solitary and contemplative, could no more do this than fly. Listen to Emerald Uthwart the schoolboy, addressing his form master just after he has had a beating from him: "And now, sir, that I have taken my punishment," he remarks in a submissive tone, "I hope that you will forgive my fault." I refuse to believe that any English schoolboy in the nineteenth or any other century, even if he were called Emerald Uthwart, ever spoke like this. Pater is no more successful when, in "A Prince of Court Painters," he sets up as a female impersonator and attempts to write an appreciation of Watteau

in the form of a diary kept by the young daughter of a
provincial bourgeois French family. The appreciation is
exquisite but the diary is as much like a real girl's diary
as Lord Fancourt Babberley was like Charlie's Aunt. As
a matter of fact such gross lapses are rare in Pater's work.
Aware perhaps that he had no dramatic gift, he generally
tries to avoid the occasion for its use. Such dramatic
incidents as his plot involves are related briefly and, as it
were, in parenthesis, after they have taken place; conversations are related in reported speech, so that Pater has
no need to try to simulate his character's tone of voice
and colloquial idiosyncrasies. These devices save him from
bathos, but at the cost of making his stories remote and
lifeless. The impression left in the memory by Marius,
and the rest of them, is that of tableaux, in which in front
of an elaborate and beautifully painted background are
posed figures beautifully and elaborately clothed, but who
are faceless, speechless and incapable of motion.

The style is the man. This is eminently true of Pater.
Not that his is a spontaneous, intimate style. On the contrary, it is as artifical as Gibbons', a studied ceremonious
affair, whose every phrase and rhythm is deliberately
fashioned to create an effect of formal hieratic beauty.
Pater seems less to be conversing than intoning; we listen
to him as to a priest intoning his daily office in some temple
dedicated to the Muses and the Graces. But the intona-
tions are unmistakably Pater's; even the reserve and the
formality are typical of him. No style is more fully
expressive of its author. This means that, in spite of the
pains he spent on it, it is not a faultless style. Like himself,
Pater's sentences are a touch languid and spiritless, and
they mirror all too accurately his nervous shrinking from
conflict. Rather than commit himself in any way that

might seem aggressive, he will hesitate, qualify, intersperse his statements with "perhaps," "almost," "somewhat," till the reader sometimes loses the thread of the argument altogether. Pater's determination to avoid ugliness at all costs leads him still further to perplex the reader. For the sake of euphony he sometimes twists and inverts the order of his sentences, so that we have to plough through two or three qualifying parentheses before we come to the main clause. Such a style is unsuitable for exposition, and still more for storytelling, for stories and arguments have to be kept moving. Pater's choice of words too can exhibit his streak of aesthete's silliness. Now and again he concentrates so exclusively on the more fanciful overtones of a word that he neglects its plain dictionary meaning. For example, in the famous passage on Mona Lisa, he represents her in the course of her mysterious peregrinations through the ages as having "trafficked in strange webs with eastern merchants." No doubt he chose the epithet "strange" because he wanted to suggest the exotic romance involved in such a transaction. But the word "strange" also means "odd." Though Pater may not remember this, the reader does, and experiences a jar. "What *is* an odd web?" he asks himself. The picture which arises in his mind is not a romantic one. The fact is that in his choice of words, as in his construction of sentences, Pater was liable to fall into the besetting sin of the conscious stylist. Like Henry James, like James Joyce, he was so anxious to write in accordance with his own ideal of the perfect style that he forgot it is a writer's first obligation to communicate his meaning to his readers.

All the same his style does cast its spell. His intelligence

appears in the winnowed concentration of his phrasing,
his sensibility in the refinement of his sense of language,
and in the slow, intricate melody of his cadences, which,
even at his most impassioned, never, as in so much fine
writing, slip into a recurrent rhythm so as to become a
sort of uneasy verse, but always retain the specific music
of prose. Pater's writing is never ugly or slipshod or
diffuse. Or undistinguished; his every sentence exhales a
perfume as strong and unmistakable as the scent of a
gardenia flower; and with some of the same languorous,
compelling sweetness. May I quote an example to you
from his appreciation, "The School of Giorgione" in
The Renaissance:

It is to the law or condition of music, as I said, that all
art like this is really aspiring; and, in the school of Giorgione, the perfect moments of music itself, the making
or hearing of music, song or its accompaniment, are themselves prominent as subjects . . . In sketch or finished
picture, in various collections, we may follow it through
many intricate variations—men fainting at music; music
at the pool-side while people fish, or mingled with the
sound of the pitcher in the well, or heard across running
water, or among the flocks; the tuning of instruments;
people with intent faces, as if listening, like those described by Plato in an ingenious passage of the *Republic*,
to detect the smallest interval of musical sound, the smallest undulation in the air, or feeling for music in thought
on a stringless instrument, ear and finger refining themselves infinitely, in the appetite for sweet sound; a momentary touch of an instrument in the twilight, as one
passes through some unfamiliar room, in a chance company.

In these then, the favourite incidents of Giorgione's school, music or the musical intervals in our existence, life itself is conceived as a sort of listening—listening to music, to the reading of Bandello's novels, to the sound of water, to time as it flies. Often such moments are really our moments of play, and we are surprised at the unexpected blessedness of what may seem our least important part of time; not merely because play is in many instances that to which people really apply their own best powers, but also because at such times, the stress of our servile, everyday attentiveness being relaxed, the happier powers in things without are permitted free passage, and have their way with us. . . .

But when people are happy in this thirsty land water will not be far off; and in the school of Giorgione, the presence of water—the well, or marble-rimmed pool, the drawing or pouring of water, as the woman pours it from a pitcher with her jewelled hand in the *Fête Champêtre*, listening, perhaps, to the cool sound as it falls, blent with the music of the pipes—is as characteristic, and almost as suggestive, as that of music itself. And the landscape feels, and is glad of it also—a landscape full of clearness, of the effects of water, of fresh rain newly passed through the air, and collected into the grassy channels.

Or listen to this passage from Pater's most poetic and original single study, "The Child in the House," where, anticipating Proust, he describes how early impressions operate, as it were, subconsciously to shape and colour his boy hero's taste and temperament.

I have remarked how, in the process of our brain-building, as the house of thought in which we live gets itself together, like some airy bird's-nest of floating thistle-down and chance straws, compact at last, little accidents have their consequence; and thus it happened that, as he walked one evening, a garden gate, usually closed, stood open; and lo! within, a great red hawthorn in full flower, embossing heavily the bleached and twisted trunk and branches, so aged that there were but few green leaves thereon—a plumage of tender, crimson fire out of the heart of the dry wood. The perfume of the tree had now and again reached him, in the currents of the wind, over the wall, and he had wondered what might be behind it, and was now allowed to fill his arms with the flowers—flowers enough for all the old blue-china pots along the chimney-piece, making fête in the children's room. Was it some periodic moment in the expansion of soul within him, or mere trick of heat in the heavily-laden summer air? But the beauty of the thing struck home to him feverishly; and in dreams all night he loitered along a magic roadway of crimson flowers, which seemed to open ruddily in thick, fresh masses about his feet, and fill softly all the little hollows in the banks on either side. Always afterwards, summer by summer, as the flowers came on, the blossom of the red hawthorn still seemed to him absolutely the reddest of all things; and the goodly crimson, still alive in the works of old Venetian masters or old Flemish tapestries, called out always from afar the recollection of the flame in those perishing little petals, as it pulsed gradually out of them, kept long in the drawers of an old cabinet.

This is Pater at his most eloquent; it is also Pater at his most creative. For, though he was no storyteller, there is a strain in his work which reveals him as a creative writer, in the strictest, fullest meaning of the word. Not only did he appreciate the principle of beauty as manifested in the work of others, he added to theirs a manifestation of his own. As no one else before or since, he has put into words the scholar's distinctive sense of the beautiful, the aesthetic emotion as it is experienced by learned, refined, and meditative spirits: and he has done this not in mere arid, intellectual statement, but distilled by the intensity with which his imagination apprehended it, into a phase of feeling, a pervading mood—the Paterian mood we may fairly call it—which saturates his most memorable passages and leaves its perfume on every page he writes. It is a mood of reverie—intent, trancèd reverie—attainable it would seem only in tranquil and immemorial surroundings, where the spirit feels itself cloistered and sealed off from the din and flux and pressure of the active world. But though it is a cloistered mood there is nothing ascetic about it. It is relaxed, receptive; and the senses, so far from being suppressed, are tremblingly awake to respond, as they could not except in tranquillity, to the subtlest and most fleeting impressions; to the play of light and shadow on running water, the flutter of a rose petal to the grass, a snatch of song heard faintly in the distance, a waft of scent from the lime trees borne on the warm windless air of a summer afternoon. Nor is Pater's response to these things a mere movement of light, indifferent pleasure. They come to him murmurous with imaginative overtones, heavy with evocative memories—of pictures, books, bygone ages, his own past—all mingling dreamily together to flood the soul, if only for a moment, with a sense of timeless beauty.

21 DAY BOOK

This book may be kept
for 21 days only
It cannot be renewed

DISCARDED
from
New Hanover County Public Library

820.4   Cecil, <u>Lord</u> David
C   The fine art of reading.

Wilmington Public Library
Wilmington, N. C.

RULES

~~1. Books marked 7 days may be kept one week. Books marked 14 days two weeks. The latter may be renewed, if more than 6 months old.~~

~~2. A fine of two cents a day will be charged on each book which is not returned according to the above rule.~~ No book will be issued to any person having a fine of 25 cents or over.

3. A charge of ten cents will be made for mutilated plastic jackets. All injuries to books beyond reasonable wear and all losses shall be made good to the satisfaction of the Librarian.

4. Each borrower is held responsible for all books drawn on his card and for all fines accruing on the same.